'A lively and opinionated chronicle, unencumbered by notions of political correctness ... *The Age of Napoleon* has interesting nuggets of information on nearly every page'

Adrian Tahourdin, *TLS*

'My favourite book of 2004 is Alistair Horne's *The Age of Napoleon*, a slim, elegant survey of the 25 years Napoleon dominated France. Horne conjures up Napoleon's world with an eye for revealing details – such as the fact that the Empress Josephine owned only two pairs of knickers'

Lucy Moore, *Mail on Sunday*

'Excellent ... deals with every aspect of the tyrant's career other than the brutal wars he imposed on his neighbours and indeed on his own people'   Claus von Bulow, *Catholic Herald*

'Vibrant ... *The Age of Napoleon* is a cultured, enjoyable introduction to the man and the mark he left on France. Horne sports his research lightly, the pigments of his narrative and illustration are vivid, the vignettes swiftly and confidently drawn, the evocation of *moeurs* knowing'

BBC History Magazine

'Horne gets the essentials of Napoleon right'

Robert Stewart, *Spectator*

'Accessible and an interesting read'   *Glasgow Herald*

Alistair Horne's work has been translated into ten languages, and he is the author of many bestselling books. They include *The Price of Glory: Verdun 1916*; *The Fall of Paris: The Siege and the Commune 1870–71*; *Napoleon: Master of Europe 1805–1807*; *A Savage War of Peace: Algeria 1954–1962*; *How Far From Austerlitz? Napoleon 1805–1815*; *Seven Ages of Paris* and, in 2004, *The Age of Napoleon* and *Friend or Foe: An Anglo-Saxon History of France*. He was knighted in 2003 for services to Franco-British relations.

By Alistair Horne

Back into Power
The Land is Bright
Canada and the Canadians
The Price of Glory: Verdun 1916
The Fall of Paris: The Siege and the Commune 1870–71
To Lose a Battle: France 1940
The Terrible Year: The Paris Commune, 1871
Death of a Generation
Small Earthquake in Chile
Napoleon: Master of Europe 1805–1807
The French Army and Politics 1870–1970
A Savage War of Peace: Algeria 1954–1962
Macmillan: 1894–1956
Macmillan: 1957–1986
A Bundle from Britain
How Far from Austerlitz? Napoleon 1805–1815
Seven Ages of Paris
The Age of Napoleon
Friend or Foe: An Anglo-Saxon History of France

The Lonely Leader: Monty 1944–45
(*with David Montgomery*)

Telling Lives
(*as editor*)

THE AGE OF NAPOLEON

Alistair Horne

PHOENIX

For David and Shiela

A PHOENIX PAPERBACK

First published in Great Britain in 2004
by Weidenfeld & Nicolson
This paperback edition published in 2005
by Phoenix,
an imprint of Orion Books Ltd,
Orion House, 5 Upper St Martin's Lane,
London WC2H 9EA

1 3 5 7 9 10 8 6 4 2

A CIP catalogue record for this book
is available from the British Library.

ISBN 0 75381 862 0

Typeset in Great Britain by
Butler and Tanner Ltd, Frome and London

Printed and bound in Great Britain by
Clays Ltd, St Ives plc

www.orionbooks.co.uk

Contents

Illustrations

Chronology

1804   Cadoudal conspiracy
       Coronation of Napoleon I
       The First Empire

1805   War of the Third Coalition
       Battle of Ulm
       Battle of Trafalgar
       Battle of Austerlitz

1806   War against Prussia and Austria
       Battle of Jena-Auerstädt

1807   Battle of Eylau
       Battle of Friedland
       Peace of Tilsit

1808   Peninsular War begins

1809   Battle of Wagram

1810   Napoleon marries Marie-Louise

1812   Invasion of Russia
       Borodino

1813   German War of Liberation (War of the Fourth Coalition)
       Battle of Dresden
       Battle of Leipzig

1814   *Patrie en Danger* campaign
       Napoleon exiled to Elba
       Congress of Vienna

1815   The Hundred Days
       Battle of Waterloo

1816   Second Bourbon restoration

SCOTLAND

*North
Sea*

IRELAND

RUSSIA

Copenhagen

Baltic
Sea

Tilsit

HELIGOLAND

Danzig

ENGLAND

London

Hamburg

PRUSSIA

Berlin

DUCHY OF
WARSAW

Amsterdam
Rotterdam

English Channel

Boulogne

Antwerp

Frankfurt

CONFEDERATION
of the RHINE

Breslau

Lille

Seine R.

Paris

Baden

Lunéville

Strasbourg

Danube R.

Vienna

• Austerlitz

AUSTRIAN
EMPIRE

Rennes

*Bay
of
Biscay*

FRANCE

Poitiers

SWITZ.

ITALY

• Budapest

• Milan

Venice

Campo Formio

Bordeaux

Rhône R.

Genoa

Toulouse

Marseilles

*Ligurian
Sea*

Leghorn

Rome

Adriatic Sea

OTTOMAN
EMPIRE

• Cattaro

Toulon

ELBA

SPAIN

CORSICA

NAPLES

CORFU

SARDINIA

Naples

M e d i t e r r a n e a n   S e a

SICILY

IONIAN ISLANDS

MALTA

N

W   E

S

France in 1789

France after the treaty
of Lunéville – 1801

French Empire in 1812

Introduction: The Age of Napoleon

A recent French book, yet one more addition to the total of over 600,000, bears the title *L'Episode Napoléonien*. Certainly it was an 'episode' that fundamentally changed Western civilisation. More embracingly, we speak of the 'Age of Napoleon' or 'The World of Napoleon'. But what dates should one set on his world, or his age? Does it begin with his birth, in 1769? No, too early; obviously the Napoleonic influence was not yet even a promise of things to come. Does it end with his fall, Waterloo and St Helena, in 1815? No, too soon; his influence carried on, like a rolling stone. Or 1821, his glum death? But what about all those lost years, imprisoned, dying of boredom, cold – possibly arsenic – in St Helena? Or what about 1840, his reinterment in state in the Invalides? But then a new Age of Napoleon, of his nephew, Louis-Napoleon, was just about to begin. And yet the influence of Napoleon I, *Napoléon le Grand*, would continue long after even the demise of his nephew.

Here I decided to risk confining the Age of Napoleon to the twenty-five years, a generation, which embraced both his zenith and his decline, from 1795, when the young general received his first post with major political elbow-power attached, to 1820 – a date by which his personality had been gone for five years, but when his influence was still strong under a shaky Restoration. And what a twenty-five years they were!

Having already written two books largely devoted to Napoleon's military career, *Master of Europe, Napoleon 1805–1807* and *How Far from Austerlitz? Napoleon 1805–1815*, and several chapters on his influence on Paris in my *Seven Ages of Paris*, I was able to concentrate here on his non-military contributions, remarkable as they were and leaving an impact far beyond the frontiers of France.

Parallels have frequently been drawn between Hitler and Napoleon, the two great warlords. But they are spurious. In terms of civil, non-military accomplishments, Hitler after twelve years in power bequeathed to Germany nothing but a mountain of skulls and rubble. Napoleon, on the other hand, had he never fought a single battle, would still have to be rated one of history's great leaders for the system of administration and the civil reforms he left behind him in France.

I The Will to Power

At the age of six I wanted to be a cook. At seven I wanted to be
Napoleon. And my ambition has been growing steadily ever since.

Salvador Dalí

How, first of all, was it possible for a poor Corsican boy, born
with limited horizons, to scale such heights? By the time he
had reached the raft at Tilsit in 1807, dictating terms to the
Tsar of All the Russians, which represented the peak of all his
military successes, he was still only thirty-seven. Because of his
youth at the conclusion of that most famous run of victories,
one tends to forget that he was born under the reign of Louis
XV and started his military career under Louis XVI. If he was a
child of the *ancien régime*, he was also very much a product of
that event dubbed by Thomas Carlyle 'the Death-Birth of a
World'. He was steeped in the French revolutionary heritage,
without which he would surely never have got as far as Tilsit.

Commissioned as a second lieutenant in 1785 at the age of
sixteen, from the harsh military academy of Brienne, somewhat
derided as a 'skinny mathematician', this scion of the lesser
Corsican nobility made his first real mark on military affairs
some eight years later, at the siege of Toulon in 1793. The key
naval base was then held by an English fleet under the command
of Admiral Hood; Napoleon, as a twenty-four-year-old artillery
captain, was brought in to advise the not very distinguished
commander of the French revolutionary forces besieging it. With
his genius for the swift *coup d'œil*, which was later to stand
him in such good stead, young Napoleon Bonaparte's strategy
succeeded, and the British were driven out. Napoleon became a
hero in the ranks of the incompetent revolutionary army

(though still unknown outside it), and was promoted to the dizzy rank of *général de brigade* when still only twenty-four, and made artillery commander to the Army of Italy.

After a brief, fallow period of considerable frustration, his next opportunity came when, by chance, he happened to be in Paris on sick leave during the autumn of 1795. A revolt was pending against the Convention and Napoleon was called in by his friend and protector, Paul Barras (one of the five members of the governing Directoire), to forestall it. He positioned a few guns (brought up at the gallop by a young cavalry captain called Murat) on the key streets leading to the Tuileries Palace. Three years previously he had witnessed the mob storm the same palace, and the weakness of the king on that occasion had made a lasting impression on him. 'If Louis XVI had shown himself on horseback, he would have won the day,' Napoleon wrote to his brother Joseph. He was determined not to repeat the same error and showed no hesitation in giving the order to fire. Discharged at point-blank range, the historic 'whiff of grapeshot' of the *Treizième Vendémiaire* put the mob convincingly to flight. For the first time since 1789 the Paris 'street' which had called the tune throughout the revolution had found a new master whom it would not lightly shrug off. Barras, grateful but also nervous at having Napoleon too near the centre of power, now appointed him – at the age of twenty-seven – Commander-in-Chief of the French Army of Italy.

Ever since 1792, France had been at war with the First Coalition of her enemies, who were bent upon reversing the revolutionary tide that seemed to threaten all Europe, and restoring the *status quo ante* in France. As Thomas Carlyle saw it, the guillotining of Louis XVI 'has divided all friends; and abroad it has united all enemies'; on the other hand, in the view of Friedrich Engels and others, had it not been for the stimulating effect of foreign intervention, the revolution might quietly have choked on its own vomit. The fortunes of war had swung back and forth; lack of adequate preparation and incompetence among the new leaders of the revolutionary French forces had been matched by differences of interest and lethargy among the Allies; the stiff forms of eighteenth-century warfare, unaltered since the days of Frederick the Great, had encountered a new revolutionary fervour, but it was poorly supported with guns and equipment. Marching into France, the Duke of Brunswick and his Prussians were halted and turned about, surprisingly, by the cannonade at Valmy in September 1792, first harbinger of a new form of warfare.

In 1793 the French forces, resurgent under the organisational genius of Lazare Carnot (whom even Napoleon was to rate 'the organiser of victory'), and fired by their first victories to carry the revolution to all the 'oppressed nations' of Europe, swept into Belgium and threatened Holland. By June 1794, Jourdan had chased the last Coalition soldier across the French frontier. The British bungled a landing at Quiberon Bay, while – defeated, and invaded in its turn – Prussia abandoned the First Coalition the following year. But, over-extended, under-equipped and unhelped by the dithering and corrupt rule of the Directoire, France's new Army of the Sambre-and-Meuse now experienced a series of defeats across the Rhine at the hands of the Austrians.

It was at this point that Napoleon was sent to Italy by Barras to wrest the initiative from the Austrians. He found the army unpaid, hungry, poorly equipped and on the verge of mutiny. Stendhal cites the example of three officers who owned but one pair of shoes, one pair of breeches and three shirts between them; elsewhere in *The Charterhouse of Parma*, he relates how, at Napoleon's legendary action on the bridge at Lodi, another French officer had the soles of his shoes 'made out of fragments of soldiers' caps also picked up on the field of battle'. By his extraordinary capacity to inspire, Napoleon totally transformed the forces under him within a matter of days, and over the next eighteen months caused them – with minimal resources – to win a series of victories. These ended with the battle of Rivoli, as impressive a battle as any the world had yet seen. By October 1797, he had captured 160,000 prisoners and over 2000 cannon, and chased the Austrians to within a hundred miles of Vienna. Here, for the first but not the last time, he forced the beaten Austrians to sign peace with France, thus marking a definitive end to the wars of the First Coalition.

The victorious young general now became the idol of France, his star irresistibly in the ascendant as he returned in triumph to Paris. 'You are the hero of all France,' the Directoire told him. Even his recently married Josephine was dubbed *Notre-Dame des Victoires* on the streets of Paris. 'From that moment,' Napoleon wrote after the first Italian campaign, 'I foresaw what I might be. Already I felt the earth flee from beneath me, as if I were being carried into the sky.' In France, now, one man and one man alone could claim a prestige that was unsullied. For France – and for Europe – it signified that the war party had triumphed.

Following Napoleon's Italian victories, at the Treaty of Campo Formio (17 October 1797), France was ceded Belgium and control of the left bank of the Rhine. Henceforth the Belgians were 'as much French as the Normans, the Alsatians, the people of Languedoc or Burgundy'. But could the English ever be persuaded to accept this notion of a French Belgium? In return for Venice and its territories, Austria recognised France's establishment of an Italian satellite state, the Cisalpine Republic, from which seed, eventually, was to germinate the modern united nation of Italy. Of her foes of the First Coalition, only England remained at war with France, but with no weapon to strike at her across the Channel; so she contented herself by extending her empire at the expense of both enemy and allies. After Campo Formio, however, in exchange for a durable peace, England too declared herself ready to accept France's 'natural frontiers' and even to hand back colonies captured during the past hostilities. At last, it seemed, revolutionary France was offered the security for which she had fought so passionately for the previous five years; it looked like a good time to make peace with England.

Nothing succeeds like success, however, and it now went to the weak head of the Directoire. But Napoleon discreetly – and temporarily – now made himself invisible, out of sight of Frenchmen who feared the advent of a Cromwell. He remarked at this time: 'Great events hang by a thread. The able man turns everything to profit, neglects nothing that may give him one chance more; the man of less ability, by overlooking just one thing, spoils the whole.'

Back in 1790, the Constituent Assembly had declared a noble ideal: 'The French nation renounces the undertaking of any war with a view to making conquests, and it will never use its forces against the liberty of any people.' But, not unlike the heirs to Lenin in the twentieth century, the Directoire, inflated by Napoleon's achievements, now let itself be enticed into graduating from a basically defensive war, with an aim of saving the revolution and securing France's frontiers, to one of expansion and enrichment. It is instructive that France's wars of aggrandisement began, not under the Consulate or the Empire, but under the revolutionary movement.

In France, the new hero was put in command – briefly – of the Army of England, charged with carrying the war across the Channel. The previous year, 1797, General Hoche with 14,000 troops and sixteen ships of the line had made an abortive descent on Ireland, which had been disrupted by storms. After an inspection in January 1798 of the 120,000 troops mustered between Etaples and Walcheren for an invasion attempt, Napoleon abandoned the idea, it being 'too chancy to risk *la Belle France* on the throw of a dice'. Instead, he placed in the mind of the

Directoire the idea of striking at British sea-power by a campaign in Egypt, and in the eastern Mediterranean – the key to England's empire and trade in the Orient.

With England's Pitt still under the misapprehension that Napoleon was heading for Ireland, he sailed for Egypt. His strategic intent was to sever at a stroke England's lifeline to her empire in India, and then – like Alexander the Great – move on to regain French possessions and conquer India itself. Had he succeeded, it would have been a historic if not a decisive event, but it was to prove, militarily, his most disastrous campaign to date. The naval failure would dog him all the way to Trafalgar.

Ensuing operations followed the familiar course, with Napoleon winning round after round on land, such as at the battle of the Pyramids, where he declared with high melodrama, 'Soldiers! Forty centuries behold you!', and with Nelson sweeping the seas at the battles of Aboukir Bay and the Nile. The fighting moved up into Palestine and the Levant, and in his massacre of prisoners at Jaffa Napoleon revealed himself at his most ruthless and cruel. The twenty-nine-year-old, who had recently issued inspiring instructions for the creation of an Institute of Science and Art in occupied Cairo – this man of so many contradictions – now gave orders to quell insurgents by 'levelling the Grand Mosque' and 'slicing off the heads of all prisoners caught in arms'. His own forces were decimated by plague, to which Napoleon himself seemed miraculously immune, and the revolutionary General Kléber growled that he was 'the kind of general who needed a monthly income of ten thousand men'. Encouraged by British naval successes, before the end of 1798 a Second Coalition comprising England, Naples, Austria, Russia and Turkey had come into being, and had begun to threaten the French position in both northern Italy and the Netherlands.

Meanwhile, news reached Napoleon that at home the wobbly Directoire was in deep political trouble. Abandoning his battered army in the Middle East and dodging Nelson's patrols, Napoleon hastened back to France, landing secretly at Fréjus on 9 October 1799. In Paris, he found the Directoire tottering. A brief moment of historic indecision followed, when it was not certain whether his grenadiers would support him or arrest him, until Murat shouted 'Vive la République!' and 'Vive Bonaparte!' On 9 November (8 Brumaire in the revolutionary calendar) Napoleon effected a *coup d'état* that ended the rule of the Directoire. 'Hypocrites, intriguers!' he castigated them, promising that he would 'abdicate from power the instant the Republic is free from danger'. He then established himself as First Consul, with a tenure of ten years and dictatorial powers greater than those of Louis XIV at the height of his glory. Both within France and beyond, this was heralded as signifying the end of the revolution.

At home no one disputed the legality of the new regime. In the words of French historian André Maurois, 'France had not been raped; she had yielded.' Tactfully, the new master now dressed himself in civilian clothes to stress the fact that, rather than rule as a general, his priority would be in domestic issues. In Russia, the mad Tsar Paul, already at odds with his Austrian ally over Italy, withdrew from the Coalition; in France, even the critical Mme de Staël was delighted, though her father, the banker Necker, cautioned: 'Your nerves are overwrought ... unfortunately, everything rests on the life of one man.'

The war, however, still continued. Consolidated in power politically, Napoleon set off once more to chastise the Austrians. By an astonishing feat of transporting an army of 50,000 secretly over the eight-thousand-foot Great St Bernard Pass, still covered in snow in the May of 1800, Napoleon struck the unwary Austrians from the rear. June brought him his stunning victory at Marengo, north of Genoa. It was a copy-book classic of manoeuvre; though, as was characteristic of Napoleon, the panegyrical bulletin he issued afterwards (aimed in part at further terrifying a demoralised foe) made it sound rather more a calculated result than was actually the case, and disallowed the element of opportunism that had played an integral part in the victory, as it so often did with his triumphs. It was a small consolation that, the following summer, General Abercromby's British expeditionary force was to defeat Napoleon's abandoned Army of the Orient and expel the last Frenchman from Egypt, for the Second Coalition had now collapsed in ruins.

The losers were punished in the peace, with the Austrians forced out of most of northern Italy, and a smarting England agreeing to part with most of her recent colonial acquisitions, including Malta. Napoleon was left, for the time being, in unchallenged military supremacy; and a grateful France confirmed him Consul for life – in a plebiscite, by a huge majority of 3.5 million to 8,000. On the other hand, Nelson at Copenhagen (2 April 1801) had once again demonstrated to Napoleon the impotence of his attempts to gain control of the seas.

Neither side was particularly happy with the peace terms, England deeply concerned by Napoleon's hegemony over Europe and resentful at her territorial deprivations, and France soon finding England in default for not withdrawing her forces from Malta. Nevertheless, for the first time in a decade, a glimmer of lasting peace flickered over the battered European nations, and, once again, it looked like as good a time as any for bringing the sequence of wars to a definitive end. But peace was to prove illusory. As Napoleon had written prophetically to his lieutenant and potential rival, Moreau, during the more ecstatic moments of 1800: 'Greatness has its beauties, but only in retrospect and in the imagination.'

Following Marengo, Napoleon had planned to enter Paris without warning. At this stage in his career he mistrusted any kind of pomp and circumstance, so, averse to a 'parade' entry, he crept into the city gates almost stealthily at 2 a.m. on 2 July.

Popular enthusiasm, however, carried all before it. To his great surprise, on his arrival at the Tuileries a dense crowd converged on the palace. Bonaparte had to show himself several times on the balcony 'amid a tempest of cries of joy'. According to one historian, 'never since Henri IV, had a conqueror been so triumphally fêted, not even Condé, Turenne or Villars'. The *défilé* lasted a whole day. At night almost every house in Paris was lit up. This time at least, it was a spontaneous celebration. Moving to the Champ-de-Mars, by the *Quatorze Juillet* the fête had become an event of the people, the grass verges on both sides of the avenue filled with an immense crowd. The guard, massed in the street in front of stands full of women in *grande toilette*, presented enemy flags to the First Consul. Lucien Bonaparte made a verbose speech, accompanied by some grandiloquent and auspicious doggerel by the poet of the moment:

> Un grand siècle finit, un grand siècle commence:
> Gloire, vertus, beaux-arts, renaissez avec lui!
> O Dieu, vois à tes pied tomber ce peuple immense:
> Les vainqueurs de l'Europe implorent ton appui . . .
> Être immortel, qu'à ta lumière
> La France marche désormais,
> Et joigne à la vertu guerrière
> Toutes les vertus de la paix!

So it must have looked in this centennial moment of exhilaration, and optimism. As the First Consul went to join his colleagues on the balcony of the École Militaire, the fervid crowd surged without restraint beneath it. From that date, declares Laborie, it could be counted 'that Marengo represented the definitive conquest of Paris by Bonaparte'. His triumphal return to Paris established him as a leader who had brought peace back to a country that had suffered severely from war. Was there anything France would not do for him?

*

Over the two decades of Napoleon's astonishing career, similar parades and celebrations would mark his victories and his triumphs, the path of his rise and his fall; equally they would provide markers to his achievements for his often bedazzled, often nervous, capital. There would be his coronation as emperor, in December 1804; his triumphal entries into Paris after the stunning victories of Austerlitz and Jena in 1805–6, and the Peace-to-End-All-Wars, of Tilsit in 1807. More muted, before an increasingly sceptical and anxious Paris, would come his return from the final victory of Wagram, in 1808; then, in 1810 and 1811, the fantasia of his remarriage to Marie-Louise of Austria, followed by the birth of the precious King of Rome – his one and only heir. In the terrible year of 1812, as the tide turned against Napoleon, would come the bedraggled return from Moscow of the broken remnants of the Grande Armée; finally, 1814 and 1815 would bring triumphal entries into Paris of a very different order – those of the victorious Allies.

Once with absolute power firmly in his hands, Napoleon wasted no time in pursuing a grand reform of French society, from the top to the bottom. First things first, towards religion his attitude was pragmatic, if not decidedly cynical – asking what God could do for him, rather than what he could do for God. On his deathbed in St Helena he sent away priests come to administer the last rites. As early as 1800, with consummate clarity, he expounded:

> How can a state be well governed without the aid of religion? Society cannot exist save with inequality of fortune, and inequality of fortune cannot be supported without religion . . .
>
> It was by becoming a Catholic that I pacified the Vendée . . . If I ruled a people of Jews, I would rebuild the temple of Solomon! Paradise is a central spot whither the souls of men proceed along different roads; every sect has a road of its own.

On assuming power, he found religion in post-revolutionary France in a state of chaos, if not jeopardy. In some regions, 'refractory priests' were still hiding out as outlaws, while in Paris each church, renamed Temples of Concord, of Hymen and so on, had its own cult – to the extent that, as Robriquet remarked, among so many 'God himself must have lost his way'. The beautiful medieval church of Saint Germain l'Auxerrois had become a 'Temple of Gratitude' during the revolution, then was used for storing fodder, while even Notre-Dame, seriously defaced, narrowly escaped destruction.

Thus one of Napoleon's first, and most popular, measures on the domestic front was to reverse the strictures imposed on freedom of religion by the men of '89. Under the revolution, and continued under the Directoire, marriage had been a simple affair, usually dispatched in batches at 'decadal' temples, the churches that had been turned into public assembly halls, to the accompanying derision of crude, layabout onlookers. With divorce made equally simple, it became regarded as a short-term obligation. 'What could be more immoral', declared a contemporary, Regnaut de l'Orme, 'than to allow a man to change his wife like a coat, and a woman to change her husband like a hat?' It was the ambition of Bonaparte, the good Corsican Catholic, to make the family the pivot of society once more, so slowly the marriage tie was encouraged to regain its former significance. On the other hand, there were to be speedy marriages for soldiers on leave from the front (under almost everything Napoleon did one could discover a military relevance); and of course there would be a separate code of divorce and morality where it affected the Bonaparte family. Napoleon himself had numerous love affairs, but – true Mediterranean to the core – was loath to tolerate them in others, especially when there was any suggestion of the scandalous.

*

Aware that piety was once more fashionable, Napoleon had the synagogues reopened and decreed that churches that had been vandalised during the revolution were to be restored at a cost of some £4 million. In this last endeavour, he was by no means influenced entirely by architectural values, but also by the kind of awareness that influenced Marx with his realisation of religion being the 'opium of the people'. With his Corsican background, Napoleon never ceased to appreciate the underlying importance of the Catholic Church when it came to winning over the French nation. Up to the time of the Concordat, the Catholic world had largely worked against the Consulate, which it regarded as born of the revolution. But as the impact of the revolution and its phobic anti-religious zeal had detumesced, so it had been accompanied in the last years of the old century by a marked religious revival. This was closely linked to the new Romantic movement, as exemplified by Chateaubriand's work, *Le Génie du Christianisme*, published in 1802. Returning to France in 1800 after seven years' self-exile, Chateaubriand had been deeply shocked at the ravages still left by the revolution, particularly in its excesses of atheism: 'the ruined castles, the belfries empty of bells, the graveyards with never a cross and the headless statues of saints'.

No less sensitive to the popular mood than any spin-driven twenty-first-century politician, Napoleon in one master stroke healed the wounds that still divided France by signing a Concordat with Pope Pius VII. It was an integral part of his programme to enlist and consolidate every element of French life behind him; yet no ruler in French history was to give the Pope a harder time. Speaking to ultra-Catholic Vendéean leaders when First Consul, he made his thinking abundantly clear: 'I intend to re-establish religion, not for your sake but for mine'.

After nine months of intense secret negotiations, the Concordat, signed in July 1801, brought France back into the Roman Catholic fold. As head of state, however, Napoleon retained the right to appoint bishops, who took their oath before him. It was part of the deal that compensation was promised for ecclesiastical lands seized by the revolution; few, in fact, were actually handed back. Napoleon's conciliatory master stroke, the Concordat, remained in force for over a hundred years, until 1905, when a new bout of anti-clericalism swept France and the Church disestablished.

The Concordat re-established the Roman Catholic Church as 'the religion of the greater majority of Frenchmen'; but at the same time it clearly demarcated its spiritual and temporal powers. Meanwhile, it removed the main grievances that had kept civil war smouldering in the Vendée, and helped gain for Napoleon the sympathies of Catholics in France as well as in the subject, or about-to-be subject, nations. Although rejected by Louis XVIII's government in exile, the Concordat was supported by most of the returning émigrés, including Chateaubriand, who found a Paris where 'the émigré was returning and talking peaceably with the murderers of his nearest and dearest'.

Largely a tactical device, however, the Concordat did not imply any religious fervour in Napoleon himself. Under his regime, notes Gwynne Lewis: 'Congregations were treated to extracts taken from the Bulletins of the Grande Armée, and informed that the paths of conscription, as much as of holiness, led to Heaven.' Moreover, though the churches were to be repaired, there was no suggestion that the actual properties sequestrated by the revolution might be returned.

In 1800, Napoleon went on record with a remark about ruling 'a people of Jews'. He followed this up by expressing serious (and, by the standards of the day, most advanced) desires for a liberal-minded emancipation of French Jewry. At the bitter siege of Acre in 1797, he had issued a proclamation declaring solemnly that Jewry had 'the right to a political existence as much as any other nation', which was never to be forgotten in the Holy Land. A precursor of Balfour ahead of his time, if Napoleon had had his way in the Middle East, might it have led to realisation of Jewish aspirations in Palestine over a century before the creation of the State of Israel? On the other hand, one needs to recall what a gulf there was between Napoleon's promises to Poles and their fulfilment. Perhaps events would only have taken a similar course in the Middle East, once Napoleon's ambition of strategic victory over the British had been achieved.

On Easter Day 1802, Napoleon sealed the diplomatic *coup* of the Concordat with a grand *Te Deum* sung at Notre-Dame to celebrate the return of peace on the international front. After ten years' silence, the tenor bell in the great cathedral tolled out to proclaim the new alliance between France and the Vatican. Napoleon was solemnly received under the portico by the recently nominated archbishop. Cynics noted that, of those present, only two defrocked priests, former Bishop Talleyrand and ex-priest Fouché, knew properly how to genuflect. A representative comment on the ceremony, and what it signified, was perhaps that of a glazier across on the Île Saint-Louis: 'Ah! Now I hear the bell of Notre-Dame; I like it much better than the *canon d'alarme*!' (The more cynical remarked of the vast gathering of police and military guards that they were there solely to 'prevent God the Father from being burgled!') As trumpeters heralded details of the Concordat across Paris, Napoleon was made to appear as the champion of Catholic, *vieille France*, a hero-leader who would restore its values and repair the depredations of Robespierre. The fall of the Terror and its replacement by the inept and corrupt Directoire had left a vacuum that was moral, military and political – and into it Napoleon slid easily.

2 *Every Epoch Dreams the Next*

I had but one goal: to reunite all, reconcile all, have all hatreds forgotten, bring everyone together, gather together so many divergent elements and compose them anew in one whole: one France and one *Patrie*.

Napoleon on St Helena

It seems extraordinary in view of the horrors that were to follow, but in 1789 the first months of the revolution had been accompanied by amazing scenes of frivolity in Paris, of frenzied dancing and bacchanalia. By the time the Terror had run its course, however, the nation seemed exhausted, like 'some frenzied person who has been bled, and undergone a strict diet'. Returning from exile, Chateaubriand described the Concorde where the guillotine had held sway as still exuding 'the shabby melancholy, the deserted air of an old amphitheatre'. Yet, it was an observable fact in France that, after a revolution, wounds suffered by the towns were always somewhat slower to heal than those of the provinces. While on leave in Paris 1795, a young Napoleon wrote to his brother, Joseph, that now 'The memory of the Terror is no more than a nightmare here. Everyone appears determined to make up for what they have suffered; determined, too, because of the uncertain future, not to miss a single pleasure of the present.'

Coming so soon after all the horrors of the Terror, it did seem no less than a miracle that the Directoire, feckless and frivolous though it may have been, should have been accompanied once again by such a relaxation, even abandonment, of morals and social barriers in Paris – where, as so often, the pace of the nation was set. This loosening of moral strictures provided a kind of screen behind which both surviving victims and executioners could share oblivion of an odious and only too recent past. As Balzac was to explain several decades later, 'The overall longing for peace and tranquillity that everyone felt after the violent upheavals produced a total obliteration of the most sinister prior occurrences. History aged very quickly, its ageing accelerated by ever new and burning interests.' Suddenly Paris appeared to discover, or rediscover, 'a moneyed upper bourgeoisie clad in Greco-Roman clothing', which – in the words of a modern-day German historian, Johannes Willms – 'imitated the way the aristocracy had lived under the Old Regime'.

It could perhaps be regarded as a symptom of the times that, under the Directoire, Parisian women wore gossamer-thin blouses, the see-through effect often enhanced by damping the fabric. They took grave risks if they entered the room against a strong light. Under the Directoire, female apparel lent the appearance, if not the reality, of a far more permissive society than that swept away by the revolution, and certainly very much at odds with the prim moral code of Robespierre and his coterie. Since the ladies of the court had vanished,

> newly rich ladies have taken their place and are surrounded, as were their predecessors, by courtesans who compete with them in extravagance and extreme fashion. These sirens are in their turn courted by a swarm of fools, who used to be called *petits-maîtres* and who are now known as *merveilleux*. They talk about politics as they dance, and express their longing for the return of the monarchy as they eat ices or watch fireworks with affected boredom.

Thus wrote a former deputy, Jean-Nicolas Demeunier, to his friend, Moreau de Saint-Méry, on returning as an *émigré* to the USA in 1797. Others thought of the fashion merely as a form of distraction, not unfamiliar to Parisians, invented by a *nouveau riche* society as an antidote to boredom.

Historians might well draw political parallels with the speedy emergence, after the *Libération* of 1944, of the *résistants de la dernière minute* as the German occupiers departed. Deeper down, however, the social topography of Paris – always centre stand of the revolution, as indeed it was of the Occupation of 1940–4 – may have been only scratched. As Evangeline Bruce depicts in her engaging book, *Napoleon and Josephine*, even in prison and under the shadow of 'the Widow' (the guillotine), the life – and loves – of the *aristos* had continued with remarkable insouciance. Given the lack of any organised birth-control, it seems extraordinary that few if any children resulted from liaisons among the incarcerated.

In the eyes of Johannes Willms, 'The Paris of the rich and the Paris of the poor grew into two separate cultural and political worlds, divided by a wall of fear and mistrust.' Here was to be the source of repeated turbulence and upheaval all through the next century – and beyond. To French historians of the left, the Directoire is a sad epilogue to the revolution and left little of value behind it. And it was the Directoire, its morals and weaknesses as well as its style, which Napoleon found himself inheriting.

The country was bankrupt, inflation rampant: shoes at 5 livres in 1790 cost 200 in 1795, and 2000 in 1797. The 'little man' lay under constant pressure for not paying his taxes. As close as the forest of Bondy there were brigands, deserters and desperate aristocrats roving. Yet, in Paris, there were still the old Jacobins left over from the Terror, with their 'feathered nests' demanding that the government should honour the pensions they had gained; it was a bit like Russia after the deluge of 1989. The country at large, filled with the single urge to rebuild, was fed up with the Directoire, its plumed hats, laces and silk breeches masquerading in the Luxembourg Palace; its executive weakness, its hateful laws, such as unjust banishment. It was also ready to fall back on the old dream of French monarchs such as Charles VIII – the conquest of Italy, which Napoleon was all too willing to provide.

Whether the government called itself a Directoire or a Consulate mattered little in people's eyes. The old revolutionary fervour had largely waned, and with it came a yearning to return to the old habits, such as the twelve-month, seven-day-week calendar instead of the confusing and unpopular *decadi*. Thus, in many senses, France was ready for Napoleon. Within a week of his coming to power, the rate of exchange doubled. It took a wise American to foresee what lay ahead; as Gouverneur Morris had observed in 1795: 'I continue to think that they will fall under the domination of a single despot.'

In March 1801, Napoleon concluded the Peace of Amiens with England. What the English, smarting from defeat, uncharitably dubbed 'the peace that passeth all understanding' heralded for both France and Napoleon a halcyon period. Yet it would be the longest in the twenty years that the revolutionary and Napoleonic wars lasted. During its thirteen months, English tourists, the curious and spendthrift, and two-thirds of the House of Lords, poured across the Channel in their tens of thousands to savour the abandoned joys of post-Directoire Paris. Tickets could be purchased at Charing Cross for £5. As a Frenchman put it, with familiar superiority: 'All the idle captives of the land of fogs shook their damp wings and prepared to take their flight towards the regions of pleasure and brightness.'

With its 547,000 inhabitants to London's 850,000 at the turn of the century, physically Paris seemed to its British visitors at first sight a dilapidated place, full of foul-smelling mud and still with open sewers. Cattle were still driven through the main thoroughfares on their way to market. It was all much as it had struck visiting English over a hundred years previously, and the tourists cocked a sceptical eye at Napoleon's declared ambitions for beautifying Paris. Nevertheless, to provide wares that would satisfy their curious and greedy visitors, French goldsmiths, jewellers and makers of fancy-goods set to work night and day. In September 1802, many visiting Britons were drawn to the great industrial exhibition mounted to celebrate the revolutionary 'Year X', at which Richard Lenoir, the cotton-spinner, alone took 400,000 francs worth of orders. The gallants found their fancies much stimulated by the manifest seductiveness of the ladies of Parisian society, in those high-waisted, see-through gowns inherited from the Directoire. 'The Bishop of Durham', remarked a visiting British officer, 'would expire at seeing the dresses ... The ladies are almost quite naked.' For the returning exiles, the landscape of Paris was familiar – though there was much excited talk about the majestic new streets that the First Consul was planning – but its customs were barely recognisable. For the English tourists swarming in, as the chestnuts along the Seine sprang into frenzied blossom, it was all quite captivating.

Suddenly, it was *gai Paris*, an ideal *endroit* in which to celebrate the new millennium. Instead of bloody heads on the Concorde, the visitors rejoiced at discovering Greek goddesses naked under their gauze dresses in the Champs-Élysees. They were perhaps less impressed by their male opposite numbers, the more than faintly ridiculous *incroyables*. With their leg-of-mutton sleeves and wide lapels, carefully crumpled shirts, tight-fitting breeches and even tighter cravats, they would stroll about the filthy Paris streets regardless of the mud, in white stockings – described altogether as 'a great expense of effort to achieve a painful result'. While the Peace of Amiens lasted, the *incroyables* took to aping the latest English dandy styles.

Approvingly, a visiting American, Benjamin West, noted how in Napoleon's France there now 'appears to be one order of people, a middle class'. Those of the English visitors privileged to be invited to the First Consul's birthday celebrations were agreeably surprised by the gracious *bonhomie* with which the great man greeted them. Fanny D'Arblay was impressed how, in his face, 'Care, Thought, Melancholy and Meditation are strongly marked with so much of Character, nay, Genius and so penetrating a seriousness'. With the utmost regard for the sensibilities of his English guests, Napoleon displayed, on either side of his chimney piece, busts of Fox and Nelson. The court around him exuded a certain brilliance – 'a newly-born government', he told his secretary, 'must dazzle and astonish' – but, in contrast to the glitter of the generals and Mameluke orderlies who accompanied him on military parades, his own uniform was striking by its simplicity, reminding the visitors more of an English sea captain in undress. Could this really be the monster who, so recently, had terrorised all Europe? At home he was undoubtedly at a peak of popularity that year, and success seemed to imbue him with a new aura of security. Fox (whom Laure Junot, wife of the Governor of Paris, thought looked like a Devon farmer) was readily won over by the First Consul, observing that 'he had no idea Frenchmen could be so pleasant'. Talleyrand, on the other hand, came over – to another Briton – as 'a nasty looking dog in a coat embroidered with silver'.

Initially, before the novelty wore off, Parisians bent over backwards to be agreeable to their former foe. Paris, recorded one,

> was infatuated with the arrival of these foreigners. It was a scramble among all classes to give them the best reception. It was the height of fashion to dine and amuse them and give them balls; the women especially were enamoured of the English and had a rage for their fashions. In short, France seemed to eclipse itself before a few thousand unprofitable foreigners ...

The English visitors, too, had to admit themselves favourably impressed by appearances of life under the new regime. For it was during this fleeting period of peace that Napoleon, acting with the same speed and remarkable concentration of energy that characterised all his military operations, established the majority of the civil reforms that were to provide France with a new constitution, set her finances in order, and comprise – *inter alia* – the *Code Napoléon*: his most durable achievements.

In no way did Napoleon succeed more triumphantly than in the ambition he had declared in 1798 to rebuild Paris. Sparked by the catastrophic floods of the previous winter, which had partly inundated the Champs-Élysées, Bonaparte began by reorganising the *quais* of the Seine; he decreed, in 1802, the construction of the Quai d'Orsay, which he eventually extended all the way to the École Militaire. Grandiose plans for canals and reservoirs were laid down, providing Paris with her modern water supply; streets were renumbered on a basis that survives to the present day. Rechristened the Musée Napoléon, the Louvre was completed in 1803 to house the Italian art treasures shamelessly looted in his recent campaigns. Inevitably there would come the grandiose architecture dedicated to military conquests; the charming Arc du Carrousel and the Vendôme Column (both to commemorate the Austerlitz triumph of 1805), and the Arc de Triomphe itself (though not to be completed until the reign of Louis-Philippe). There were also works of purely economic significance, like the Bourse (the foundation stone of which was laid in 1808, although the idea was conceived by Napoleon much earlier), and the vast Halle des Vins – designed to make Paris the foremost trading centre for wine in northern Europe.

The list of works initiated is an imposing one, especially considering the short amount of time Napoleon was able to spend on the home front: the Rue de Rivoli, Rue de Castiglione, Rue Napoléon (renamed Rue de la Paix), the Conseil d'État and the Cour des Comptes, four new bridges, the Madeleine transmogrified into a Temple of Victory with, facing it across the Concorde, the portico of the Palais Bourbon remodelled in Roman style to match. Everywhere new fountains and parks were constructed, and – not least – churches that had been vandalised during the revolution were to be restored over the next twelve years.

Rapidly France began to display signs of the clock being turned back on the revolution. First of all, after coming to terms with the Church, Napoleon abolished the savage Law of Hostages, which had made the illegal return of *émigrés* punishable by death, as well as imposing harsh fines on their relatives. In 1802 he proclaimed a general amnesty for most categories of proscribed exiles. Here he was, of course, mindful of gaining the support of the monarchists for his future plans of continental conquest. As a consequence of this policy, within the first year of the Consulate over 40,000 families were permitted to return. The revolutionary *bonnet rouge* was removed from buildings and steeples. The titles of *Madame* or *Mademoiselle* once more replaced the appellation of *citoyenne*. *Citoyen*, with all its fearful associations, disappeared for ever. The revolutionary calendar of ten months disappeared in favour of the old twelve-month calendar, so that *18 Brumaire, An VII* once more became 9 November 1799; and traditional pre-revolutionary festivals like Christmas and Easter returned to fashion. Renamed 'Place des Fédérés', and then 'Place de l'Indivisibilité', under the revolution, the old Place Royale now became (and remained for ever) the Place des Vosges – for the good reason that that *département* had excelled itself in revenue contributions over the past year, and thus deserved a pat on the back. The 'Bureau des Pauvres' was closed down, on the politically correct grounds that it was considered 'humiliating'.

Masked balls had been banned by the revolutionaries; Napoleon's new Prefect of Police for Paris, Edmond-Louis-Alexis Dubois, no fun-lover he, continued the ban, but his boss, the astute Fouché – realising the PR value – rescinded the ban to allow four a year at the Opéra. Ambassadors had their proper

court costume restored; while Napoleon, in May 1802, insti-
tuted the new award of the Légion d'Honneur – a new society,
he reasoned, needed a new élite, an aristocracy not of birth, but
of merit. Boundless in his own ambition, Napoleon derided it
in others, and he remarked disdainfully of his own creation, the
Légion: 'it is by such baubles that one leads men by the nose!'
Yet he recognised full well its significance. From a charming
small palladian palace on the Left Bank, the Hôtel Salm (where
it resides today), under the Empire no less than 48,000 *rubans
rouges* were distributed, among them 1200 to civilians. The
cynics may have derided the institution as 'hanging by a thread!',
nevertheless it would continue to be a source of power and
influence for even republican regimes long after Napoleon's
demise.

And how did France's First Consul, and his consort, view the
'peace that passeth all understanding'? During those brief years,
the prospects for France looked rosier than they ever had. In
retrospect, it would certainly seem like one of the nation's
Golden Ages – comparable to the advent of Henri IV, or Louis
XIV after the defeat of the Fronde. According to Evangeline
Bruce, both Napoleon and Josephine would remember those
two years as the 'happiest time of their lives'. They had Malmaison, only an hour's drive out of Paris (rather more now). If
their idyll at Malmaison says something about their brief weeks
of peace together, it also reflects the country life of the affluent
and comfortable French at the turn of the nineteenth century.
Desperately wanting to become a *grand seigneur*, Bonaparte had
tried to buy land contiguous to his small-holding at Malmaison.
But neighbours refused, so he had to be content with a parcel of
300 acres of woodland, fields and vineyards, a working farm
running down to the poplar-fringed Seine – for which he paid
ff325,000.

'Because of the freshness of the Seine,' recorded Mme de

Rémusat, 'nothing could be fresher or greener than the fields and park of Malmaison.' Here Josephine had her Damietta roses (named after the campaign in Egypt), and the painting of them by the great Redouté – and her famous Egyptian gazelles to which Bonaparte had a habit of feeding his snuff. Though in essence it remained an unpretentious, and charming, country house, Josephine, always extravagant, filled it with priceless paintings and marbles questionably acquired by the Bonapartes in Italy, and progressively expanded it. (Allegedly Bonaparte had 'pocketed' ff4 million extorted from the city of Hamburg, in 1800, in order to refurbish Malmaison and pay Josephine's debts.) At the entrance was erected a metal awning painted to resemble the striped canvas of an army bivouac. On police chief Fouché's insistence, barracks six times larger than the residence itself were built for the consular guard.

Inside, most of the rooms on the ground floor had (and still have) a distinctly martial flavour. His Salle de Conseil (small, reflecting the small number of his entourage from whom Napoleon ever felt in need of counsel) was decorated like a campaign tent, full of symbolic eagles and macho winged lions, and hung with emblems of war. The salon is dominated by very square, military-style consoles by Desmalter, his favourite cabinet-maker. Even the *bibliothèque*, as so often in the eighteenth and nineteenth centuries the most charming room in the house, with its gently curved walls, is dominated by fasces and helmeted Roman centurions blasting trumpets. Here Napoleon would work happily at a table on which he kept a model of the *Muiron*, the ship in which he had escaped from Egypt. Everywhere the influence of Egypt, the sphinxes and lions' feet, is evident. Upstairs even Josephine's bedroom pays homage to Mars by being enveloped in a tent – though, a concession to her femininity, the colours are deep rose with an oval blue sky. Elegant gilt swans support the bedhead (Napoleon's, in contrast, displays Roman heads and lions' feet).

Napoleon liked to work out of doors, and in summer a little tent containing a desk and a chair was set up for him on a bridge over the lake. He claimed that, in the open air, his ideas became 'more elevated and expansive'. His Corsican blood could endure no cold, and fires were lit indoors even in July. In the evenings their principal pastime was the theatre, which Josephine had ordered constructed to seat some 200. Even Talma was invited down to run productions, and all the entourage was expected to act. Napoleon's new secretary, Méneval, recorded that 'The only other place I have found Bonaparte as contented as he was on a battlefield, was in the gardens at Malmaison.' Bourrienne, his predecessor and Napoleon's old school friend, brutally dumped by him, wrote acidly that there 'He had everything required … to be a pleasant man, except the wish to do so.'

Though she complained about the discomfort of the bedrooms on the second floor, with their cold bare red tiles, seventeen-year-old Laure Junot, wife of one of Napoleon's generals (then Governor of Paris, his nickname *La Tempête*), recorded: 'We led a merry life, and the summer slipped pleasantly away.' That is, until the future Emperor made a pass at her. Out of the gaze of Josephine, and while *La Tempête* was away in Paris, he took to visiting her at dawn – and pinching her toe provocatively. On the third night, she locked herself in, but Napoleon found a master key. Then she persuaded her husband to stay overnight. The following morning, Napoleon was surprised to find Junot in her bed at breakfast time, but recovered his composure to declare that his general was 'A better alarm clock than myself!' 'Faith! *that is an admirable man!*' the evidently simple-minded Junot remarked. Finding the pressure at Malmaison now unbearable, Laure fled to Paris. Junot was never made a marshal.

According to the disenchanted Bourrienne, Bonaparte's departures from Malmaison were noted by practically everybody with pleasure: 'Everyone breathed more easily, became more cheerful in the absence of the master … All changed again immediately upon his return.' Nevertheless, Malmaison undoubtedly represented the 'happiest times' in Napoleon and Josephine's life together, and they spent as much of it as possible there. They had each other, in that longest period of peace in the Napoleonic Wars, and it was also the longest time they would spend together. At Malmaison also Napoleon had a better chance of keeping the voracious sexual appetite of the hot-blooded Creole under control; she could even keep a reasonable tab on his passing infidelities. Anyway, she loved it; Malmaison was Josephine's 'creation and her paradise'. So it remains today, though the roses seem neglected, and some disrepair hangs over Malmaison. Its shutters removed, the frontage looks bleak, reflecting the general air of sadness. Discarded and alone, Josephine would die there in 1814 while Napoleon was in exile in Elba. In June 1815, bound for his last exile after Waterloo, he made a tearful farewell visit there, lamenting: 'My poor Josephine! I can see her now, walking along one of the paths and picking the roses she loved so well ... We never really had any quarrels except about her debts.'

And then they had the Tuileries. After a hundred days spent in Marie de Médicis' Palais du Luxembourg, in the spring of 1800 they moved in to the great palace that stretched across the Louvre. Josephine was not happy about the move. 'I was never made for so much grandeur,' she confessed to sister-in-law Hortense. 'I will never be happy here. I can feel the Queen's ghost [she had been dead less than ten years] asking what I am doing in her bed.' Napoleon was more robust, picking her up and carrying her off into the royal suite: 'Come on, little Creole, get into the bed of your masters!' To Napoleon residence in the Tuileries was an essential indication of the continuum of power. 'It's not enough to be here,' he remarked to Bourrienne, 'the problem will be to stay.' He declared, pointing to a nearby window, 'I watched the siege of the Tuileries from there and the capture of that good Louis XVI, but *I* will remain here!' Within less than five years, with imperial trappings, he would be cloaking the great palace with rather more than the mantle of First Consul.

By May 1803 the uneasy Peace of Amiens had run out. There was disenchantment between visitors and hosts in Paris, with one of the former complaining, in a familiar manner, how his hotelier 'in every way he could, fleeced us and, seeing no more was to be got, took no further notice of us'. It reflected the diplomatic level, where mutual accusations of bad faith between France and England began to proliferate. On 18 May 1803, Britain again declared war.

Nevertheless, under the constitution as he had amended it the previous year, Bonaparte's authoritarian rule seemed unshakeably established with virtually all wires in the nation leading back to his one pair of hands. One linchpin in the whole structure was missing, however; the continuity of succession. Already in December 1800, the fact that the First Consul might be less than immortal had been suggested when, on his way to the opera, he had narrowly escaped the explosion of a powerful mine in the Rue Niçaise, which killed several bystanders and caused much destruction near the Louvre. Josephine had been asleep; the coachman drunk. The Jacobins were implicated, although Fouché held the royalists responsible, and severe penalties were meted out. On being made Consul for life in August 1802, Napoleon was granted powers to nominate a successor, but his ambitions lay further.

Then, at the beginning of 1804, two further plots were uncovered: one led by a Vendée royalist from Brittany called Georges Cadoudal, the other by two generals, Pichegru and Moreau. Cadoudal (in whose conspiracy the Addington government in Britain had rashly connived) was swiftly picked up, near the Odéon, by that master counter-spy, Fouché. Cadoudal's involvement in the Rue Niçaise bomb was revealed, and he was executed on 25 June 1804 – along with a dozen others in one of the few mass guillotinings of the Napoleonic era. Pichegru died in prison, garrotted by his own neckerchief; while Moreau, as the popular hero of the battle of Hohenlinden, was permitted to disappear into exile, thereby removing one of the few potential rivals to Napoleon. (Becoming military adviser to the Tsar, he was to die fighting his own countrymen at the battle of Dresden, in 1813.) A Captain Wright, also caught by Fouché's men, died after a long stay in prison, in 1805, in most suspicious circumstances.

The Cadoudal plot provided Napoleon with just the excuse he needed to give himself an imperial crown, thereby ensuring the hereditary succession of the Bonaparte dynasty; but it was also to lead to his most deplorable blunder, the murder of the Duc d'Enghien. A fairly distant, and disinterested, potential claimant to the Bourbon throne, d'Enghien was an attractive young man of thirty-two who made occasional secret visits to the German state of Baden, in the pursuit of love. On one such visit he was kidnapped on Napoleon's orders and brought to France, along with his inseparable dog, for an arbitrary trial on charges of conspiracy. He was summarily shot, in the fortress of Vincennes. The faithful dog somehow survived, to become adopted by King Gustavus IV of Sweden; on its collar read the inscription 'I belong to the unhappy Duc d'Enghien'. Totally innocent, d'Enghien was unaware even that any conspiracy against the First Consul existed.

The shots rang around Europe; in the famous phrase attributed (wrongly) to Talleyrand, whose own hands were far from clean, the deed was 'worse than a crime, it was a blunder'. Certainly no other single act did Napoleon more harm, showing as it did what pointless evil this glamorous hero was also capable of. Combined with his forthcoming coronation, the greatest *spectacle* Napoleonic Paris was ever to see, the two events would be fundamental in the launching of the Third Coalition against France. 'We have achieved more than we intended,' declared the royalist conspirator, Georges Cadoudal, with acid humour as he courageously faced the scaffold in June 1805. 'We came to give France a king; we have given her an emperor.'

Though the Directoire had done much to improve France's political structure, between 1799 and 1804 the constitution was extensively remodelled by Napoleon; of course greatly to the increment of his own personal power. To lend legitimacy to his amendments he utilised the instrument of the plebiscite (one to which Charles de Gaulle, a century and a half later, was also to resort). The resulting votes always came up with resounding majorities for the First Consul, not unlike those of Soviet regimes in the twentieth century. Occasionally the results were fudged; nevertheless the vast majority of Frenchmen favoured anything that represented a turning away from the decade of anarchy, misrule, corruption and destruction handed down from the revolutionaries of '89. Heir to the revolution, Napoleon was however in no way himself a revolutionary, but a reformer and a moderniser prepared to graft innovations and streamlinings on to the stock of both the *ancien régime* and the few sensible benefits bequeathed by the revolution. As it did in his military technique, rationalisation lay also at the heart of all his civil reforms.

After Brumaire, much of Napoleon's attention had been directed into reorganising inefficient administrations – of which there were many. In February 1800, the various provincial *départements* were placed under the charge of prefects; the following year the metric system was introduced, and in 1802 a new national police force was raised. France was to become more tightly centralised than ever it had been under the *Roi Soleil*. Prior to Napoleon, the country had been bedevilled by the existence of 360 separate local codes; he now set about the immense task of unifying them into one set.

By 1804 the *Code Civil* (later, and better, known as the *Code*

Napoléon) was voted through the legislature. Though comprising over 2000 articles, it took only four years to complete. It remains Napoleon's most solid and enduring achievement, and is still largely operative today. Typical both of his energy and personal interest in the work of administrative reform, Napoleon managed, almost incredibly, to attend no fewer than 57 of the 109 meetings devoted to the *Code Civil*. Regulating virtually every function of life, the Code insisted on the equal division of property among sons, thereby doing more than the revolution had to fragment the big estates. Reflecting Napoleon's own, very Corsican disbelief in feminine equality, heavy emphasis was laid on the authority of the male, removing many of the contractual rights that women had enjoyed under the *ancien régime*. The *père de famille* was granted almost dictatorial rights over the family, including the right to imprison his child for a month; while illegitimates were barred from any right of inheritance. For women the Code represented a distinctly retrograde step; wives, for instance, were forbidden to give, sell or mortgage property and could acquire it only with their husband's written consent. In this respect Frenchwomen had been better off under Louis XVI, or even Louis XIV.

After the Civil Code came the Codes of Civil Procedure, Commercial Law, Criminal Procedure and the Penal Code. All embodied the key achievements of the revolution – national unity and the equality of citizens – and were to survive as the basis for the body of civil law throughout the modern world. Under the Consulate, of the three democratic institutions nominally governing France, the Tribunate could discuss proposed legislation, but not vote on it; in the Legislative Body, legislation was voted on but not discussed, while the Senate came to have no powers at all. By 1804, however, Napoleon had concentrated every aspect of power within his own hands – save a crown, and its guarantees of succession. It was, by any standard, a remarkable achievement; by the sum of his administrative contributions on the civil side he deserves to go down in history as one of its great men. As he said of his endeavours, on St Helena:

> My true glory lies not in having won forty battles, but that which nothing will efface is my *Code Civil*; the verbal proceedings of my *Conseil d'État*; the collected correspondence with my ministers; in fact, all the good that I did as an administrator, as a reorganiser of the vast *famille française* ...

Bonaparte may be accused of being an opportunist, but his supreme asset was to carry with him from Corsica no burden of class distinction or privilege. This was to help him immeasurely in founding his own elite, regardless of whether they were former aristocrats, revolutionaries or of the humblest proletarian stock. An adept psychologist, though sweeping away inherited privileges, he created bureaucratic appointments to allure former aristocrats to support him. With the old aristocracy his policy of reconciliation may have been less successful, and it continued (at least in the earlier stages, before his staggering successes began to have a look of permanence) to keep a mistrustful distance. Nevertheless, one of Napoleon's outstanding successes was his creation of an essentially classless elite, as dignified by the *Légion d'Honneur*, faithful to his person alone.

It was manifestly no exaggeration to say that every soldier of the Grande Armée marched with a marshal's baton in his knapsack. Only two of his twenty-six marshals had noble antecedents (the revolution, partly, had seen to that) and by the time of Austerlitz in 1805 half of the officer corps had risen from the ranks. The flamboyant cavalry genius, Murat, was the twelfth son of a humble Cahors innkeeper; Ney, 'the bravest of the brave', was the son of a cooper; Masséna, one of Napoleon's finest marshals, was the orphaned son of a grocer who had gone to sea as a cabin-boy at thirteen; Bernadotte rose from the ranks to become, eventually, King of Sweden; Lefebvre's wife was a washer-woman. They were also young, insofar as Napoleon reckoned that no commander had any gumption left by the time he was forty-five. But the same considerations applied throughout his civil administration.

Thus, creating his own empire nobility of 1000 barons, 400 counts, 32 dukes and 3 princes (not to mention a handful of kings from his own family), did he aim to unite France – and, of course, to further his own advantage. 'The government,' he declared in one of his earliest proclamations, 'neither wants, nor recognises parties any more, seeing in France only Frenchmen.' On St Helena he stated: 'I had but one goal: to reunite all, reconcile all, have all hatreds forgotten, bring everyone together, gather together so many divergent elements and compose them anew in one whole: one France and one *Patrie*.' In this Napoleon Bonaparte was to succeed, better than most of his predecessors, let alone successors.

As in almost every field of human endeavour, Napoleon had vigorous views on the education of Frenchmen. Under the *ancien régime* it had resided largely in the hands of village priests and religious orders. Napoleon's views on the subject were simply stated; they were essentially traditionalist, and certainly non-revolutionary. In conformity with all his other administrative reforms, his aim was to modernise and centralise education. 'Up to the present,' he declared at a session of the Council of State in 1804–5,

> the only good education we have met with is that of the ecclesiastical bodies. I would rather see the children of the village in the hands of a man who knows only his catechism, but whose principles are known to me, than of a half-baked man of learning who has no foundation for his morality and no fixed ideas. Religion is the vaccine of the imagination; she preserves it from all dangerous and absurd beliefs. An ignorant [*ignoranti*] friar knows

enough to tell a working man that this life is but a passage. If you take faith away from the people you end up producing highway robbers.

In 1795 the Directoire had introduced a new secular system on to which stem, accepting the best and rejecting the worst, Napoleon grafted, in 1802, one of the most popular and enduring of all his reforms – the *lycées*, or state secondary schools.

All schools were placed under direct supervision of the state, with funds allocated for the education in higher, specialised schools of a promising elite. Principles were applied similar to those by which he had obtained uniformity in his artillery pieces, with education organised as for the training of an army. In all France's secondary schools, for instance, it could be reckoned that the same Latin passage was being translated at the same hour. Pupils would be summoned to recitations by drum-roll – and the drums were still rolling a century later.

As with Napoleon's other administrative innovations, it was no mean task to impose a new, uniform educational system on a nation with such deep-rooted anarchic tendencies, even pre-'89. Like so many Napoleonic reforms, the system was of course designed, at least in part, to serve his own aims by providing a steady flow of military and administrative cadres essential to the Napoleonic war machine. At the same time he transformed the high-grade École Polytechnique, founded by the Convention in 1794, into a military college for gunners and engineers. He also set his seal on the École Normale Supérieure, likewise initiated by the Convention and still today the breeding ground of a particular genre of French intellectual leadership. For all the talk about *égalité*, it was however extensively elitist; by the last year of Empire there were still only thirty-six *lycées* with 9000 pupils in all France, and most of them came from the middle and upper classes.

*

As with every other function of education, Paris's Sorbonne University swiftly felt the new broom. Under the revolution the great university, its foundations laid by Abelard in the eleventh century and built upon by Richelieu in the seventeenth, had once more fallen on hard times. On account of its clerical orientations, it had received rough treatment from the revolutionaries, who stole its precious sculptures and left the university to crumble. Closed down, the Sorbonne remained empty until Napoleon took a hand in 1806. Then he established the Académie de Paris, the Faculté des Lettres, des Sciences et de Théologie in its buildings. Once again the Sorbonne thrived.

Following the fall of the Empire, it was allowed once more to fall into decay; under the Restoration arguments persisted about its rebuilding; but nothing was done, until Napoleon III and Baron Haussmann came along in the 1850s.

Typical of Napoleon's fervent intervention in cultural matters that went *pari passu* with military campaigning was the 'living encyclopedia' of scientists, geographers, orientalists, chemists, zoologists and artists, 160 strong, including Monge the great mathematician and Champollion the Egyptologist, whom Napoleon had taken with him on the expedition to Egypt. He had lost the war there, but discovered the Rosetta Stone, which eventually ended up in England. It was perhaps typical of the Napoleonic image, and myth, and of the drive and enthusiasm he injected into French culture across the board, that – although losing the campaign in Egypt, at considerable cost, and although his expedition had only spent a matter of months there – Egypt would always remain at the centre of his whole ethos, cultural as well as military. If Mary Tudor could protest that she would die with 'Calais' engraved on her heart, surely a post-mortem would have found 'Egypt' on Napoleon's. At the same time his 'living encyclopedia' would always recognise their boundless debt to him.

3   *Fortune is a Woman*

He always applied all his means, all his faculties, all his attention
to the action or discussion of the moment. Into everything he put
passion. Hence the enormous advantage he had over his adversaries,
for few people are entirely absorbed by one thought or one action at
one moment.

Caulaincourt

The great *Te Deum* of 1802 was to be but a rehearsal for the
most magnificent *spectacle* of all just a year and a half later.
2 December 1804 was a day of intense cold in Paris. But the sun
broke through the fog at 9 o'clock – just as it was to do at
Austerlitz the following year. Acting with a grandeur that was
indicative of the vast power that he had already acquired in
Europe, and in consequence of the Concordat, Bonaparte had
managed to bully the Pope, Pius VII, to come to Paris to officiate
in person and bestow the imperial crown on him at Notre-
Dame. Weary from his long journey, the Pope was obliged to
descend from his carriage and stand in the mud to be received
by Napoleon. He was then seated in an inferior position in the
imperial coach. In the talks that ensued, Napoleon is described
as alternately cajoling and threatening. The Pope, immobile
and bored, would merely comment in Italian 'comediante' and
'tragediante' as one mood replaced another. In Paris – a city only
so recently bent on expunging religion and which, even in the
days of the Most Christian Capetian Kings, had never seen a
real live Pope before – the frail, mild-mannered man, appearing
interested in everything and speaking kindly to everyone, made
the most favourable of impressions. The hardest-line Jacobins
bowed their heads before him. There was a brisk sale of rosaries –
one operator made ff40,000 that January alone – while the police

estimated that some two million persons were present in the capital for the event. As an illustration of Bonaparte's own relations with the Pope (and indeed as an indication of his true views on religion), when his brother Jérôme contracted a marriage (with an American) of which Bonaparte disapproved, he commanded Pope Pius VII to have the Catholic Church annul the marriage. Pius, still suffering from his humiliation during the coronation, refused. Napoleon retaliated by making him a prisoner. (Jerome remarried, bigamously; though made King of Westphalia, all his subsequent children remained bastards.) Napoleon's relations with the Pope were to be forever paradoxical; he would despoil him, intern him, and get himself excommunicated, yet remain the official master of France's clergy. His quarrels with the Holy See came to be looked on as 'little local difficulties' by his entourage.

At the coronation, pomp and circumstance joined hands with the ridiculous, with bystanders noting first of all that eight horses were harnessed to the great coach; a number properly reserved exclusively for royalty. 'I saw five regiments of cavalry and Mamelukes pass,' wrote the father of Aurore Dupin (who was to become better known as George Sand), in a letter to his wife:

> twelve, thirteen, fourteen carriages drawn by six horses, each full of courtiers; a carriage with ten windows full of princesses ... finally the Emperor's, eight cream-coloured horses, beautiful beasts, caparisoned and decked with pompons as high as the first storey of the houses ... On the way back there were magnificent illuminations, dances, fireworks, etc., etc. ... Goodbye to the Republic. Neither you nor I will miss it.

It was a view echoing that of many Frenchmen that day, and one that could also be repeated as subsequent French republics disintegrated.

The whole façade of the cathedral had been clad with a cardboard Gothic exterior for the occasion, provoking the comment from a wit that 'so much work has been done that God Himself would lose his bearings!' Waiting at Notre-Dame were sixty bishops with their attendant clergy, the Senate, the Legislative Body, the Council of State, princes of Nassau, Hesse and Baden – Napoleon's new allies – the Arch-Chancellor of the Holy Roman Empire and ministers of the various European powers. Closest to the Emperor were personages of the new Court, generals mostly from plebeian backgrounds. Some had been Jacobins and regicides only the previous decade, but now all bore resounding titles: Grand Chamberlains, Grand Marshals, Grand Masters of the Hounds. In the west end of the great cathedral, and opposite the altar, was raised up a platform twenty-four steps high and set between immense columns – upon it an immense throne. As he ascended the steps to it, Napoleon is said to have murmured to his brother: 'Joseph, if only our father could see us now!' Napoleon, not the Pope, elected to place the imperial crown on his own head, as Josephine knelt before him in obeissance. (Two days previously, she had persuaded Cardinal Fesch – Napoleon's uncle – to marry them secretly in the Tuileries, possibly to make her own position more secure. It would, but for a bare six years only.)

There were moments of dissonance during the coronation, which threatened to introduce farce into a scene of high majesty. To begin with, Napoleon had refused to receive Communion, being unwilling to go to confession first. Then, between the altar and the throne, a slight altercation broke out between Josephine and the jealous sisters-in-law carrying her train, with the result that she was momentarily arrested in her procession. Chagrined by receiving only two tickets for the coronation, David, the court painter with a reputation for self-promotion, sought his revenge by painting himself into the ponderous formal tableau. The *mauvaises langues*, too, whispered that the imperial coach was over-the-top; that in the attire he had chosen the hero of Marengo was unrecognisable; that the Emperor, his short, plump body encased in a bejewelled costume inspired by the huge frame of François Premier – which did not become him – ludicrously resembled the King of Diamonds.

After the coronation, although Paris danced all night in four ballrooms specially constructed in the Concorde, there were also critics in the world beyond. In Vienna, when Beethoven learnt that Napoleon had proclaimed himself Emperor, he scratched out his name from the *Eroica* in a rage. Napoleon, he is said to have exclaimed, was 'nothing more than an ordinary mortal'; he would, Beethoven predicted, 'trample on all human rights ... [and] become a tyrant'. Mme de Staël was particularly indignant: 'for a man who has risen above every throne, to come down willingly and take his place among the kings ...!' she objurgated; while young Henri Beyle (aka Stendhal) damned 'this so obvious alliance of all the charlatans. Religion coming to consecrate tyranny, and all that in the name of human happiness!'

Returning to the Tuileries, now no longer Bonaparte but henceforth Napoleon I, there was an unfortunate omen. The weighty crown toppled off the coach. In a state of *post coitum triste*, the new Emperor gloomed to his secretary the following day: 'I have come too late; men are too enlightened; there is nothing great left to do.' This was not, however, a view generally shared by the denizens of a Paris bemused by the 'bread and circuses' feat *par excellence* of free feasting and fireworks that had accompanied the dazzling occasion. It merely seemed as if Napoleon had ascended to yet another pinnacle of glory, and of these there still promised to be no end. After a four-month stay, garnering respect from every quarter, the Pope returned to Rome. A thinly veiled insult, the tiara Napoleon had presented to him for his services was encrusted with jewels that the French had looted from the Vatican in 1798; four years later Pope Pius would find himself a prisoner of Napoleon, with eight French cannon trained on his windows. Yet the coronation had been an extraordinary *fantasia* of power and sheer machismo. Europe had better tremble – and look out, now.

What kind of person was the new Napoleon I at this moment when he had vested himself in the pomp and circumstance of power comparable only to that of the Roman Caesars, of Charlemagne and of the Holy Roman Emperors? Like his fortune, the man himself now stood at his zenith both physically and intellectually. Still only thirty-five, *Le Petit Caporal* or *Le Tondu*, as the army called him affectionately, was beginning to show just a few signs of thickening; his cheeks were fuller, the waistband of his breeches tighter, his complexion sallower. Already he had been *cocu* by Josephine (and vice versa). Some of his less intimate officers thought that possibly his gaze was a trifle duller, and they would reflect apprehensively among themselves that it was now over four years since he had won that last great military victory, at Marengo; could it be that 'perhaps the crown has squashed his brains?'

They would soon be proved wrong.

Millions of words have been written about Napoleon's complex personality, re-examining its mysteries and paradoxes, and sometimes, even, manufacturing new ones. He hunted, not because he enjoyed it or was even particularly good on a horse, but because he deemed it part of the regal appanage. He espoused pageantry, insofar as it was a function of the courtly life designed to bedazzle the impressionable, but in fact was happier himself amid the almost martial simplicity that Josephine had created for him at Malmaison. He was also no gourmet; fifteen minutes, he always said, was enough for any meal – and about the same for making love. He derided ambition in others, yet was bound-less in his own. He was bred on the egalitarian ideals of the revolution, but was to found a new aristocracy and a new despotism of his own. He condemned sexual love as 'harmful to society and to the individual happiness of men', and was known to have derided it as merely 'an exchange of perspirations'; yet he was incapable himself of avoiding both its entanglements and torments of jealousy. He leaned towards mathematics and the sciences of Reason, while mistrusting anything to do with human passions; yet he could never quite escape from being a child of the Romantic Movement himself. He was (wrote George Rudé): 'a man of action and rapid decision, yet a poet and dreamer of world conquest; a supreme political realist, yet a vulgar adventurer who gambled for high stakes'. About certain facets of Napoleon's character there has been little argument. One was the extraordinary impact he had on people. 'The terror he inspires is inconceivable,' wrote his enemy Mme de Staël: 'One has the impression of an impetuous wind blowing about one's ears when one is near that man.'

As for Napoleon's relationship with his soldiers, perhaps the single most remarkable feature was the total dedication he was able to exact; the *grognards* would march to Moscow and back for him – and then, once again, pick up their muskets during the Hundred Days. Another incontrovertible asset of Napoleon was his almost superhuman reserve of energy. It was this energy that enabled him to be, so his admirer Goethe thought, 'in a permanent state of enlightenment, which is why his fate was more brilliant than the world has ever seen or is likely to see after him'. He could concentrate eighteen hours a day without his mind clouding. 'I work the whole time,' he once explained to Count Roederer. 'It is not a genie that reveals to me suddenly what I have to say or to do in a circumstance which may surprise others, it's my reflection, it's meditation.'

By the beginning of 1805, that capacity for work was certainly undiminished. So too was the retentiveness of that remarkable, questing, restless mind and Napoleon's genius for total concentration. As Caulaincourt, his trusted aide, explained:

> He always applied all his means, all his faculties, all his attention
> to the action or discussion of the moment. Into everything he
> put passion. Hence the enormous advantage he had over his
> adversaries, for few people are entirely absorbed by one thought
> or one action at one moment.

'An infinite capacity for taking pains', 'an intuitive sense', 'an indomitable will to power', 'a firmness of aim'; these are some of the many qualities attributed to Napoleon. Above all he was a man of reflexive action. A remark made in his youth revealed clearly his distrust of self-examination: 'When a man asks himself "Why do I exist?" – then in my opinion, he is the most wretched of all. His machine breaks down, his heart loses the energy that is proper to men.'

Even if it did not lead to happiness, he thought action was better than introspection, which inevitably showed the way to wretchedness. Although a Voltairean sceptic, this also applied to his religious beliefs. Such beliefs were perfectly acceptable for others (and particularly women), but where he was concerned, 'I am glad I have no religion,' he confided to his intimate, Bertrand. 'It is a great consolation I have no imaginary fears. I do not fear the future.' His mistrust of intellectualism perhaps lay at the root of his aversion to Mme de Staël and her fellow ideologues; 'They talk, talk, talk,' he complained to his brother, Lucien. Occasionally this aversion also led him into faulty conclusions, as for instance when he rejected a blueprint by the American genius, Robert Fulton, for the invention of a submarine: 'All these inventors, all these project mongers are either schemers or visionaries. Don't mention him again.'

'Men are moved by two levers only: fear and self-interest,' he once declared. To some extent he approved of Robespierre's Terror, regarding it – like the actions of a twenty-first-century terrorist – as 'one of the inevitable phases' of revolution, a process that 'can be neither made nor stopped'. In no way ashamed, for example, of his own relentless looting of treasures in Italy, he regarded the acquisition of the booty of war by his subordinates as just one of the elements comprising the lever of 'self-interest'.

It was his instinct for action that placed him on a treadmill leading, ineluctably, from one conquest to another. In terms of both strategy and tactics he did, however, also possess the rare capacity to bide his time, waiting for the *moment juste*. It was, he admitted, a characteristic to which the 'Gallic temperament' was ill-suited: 'yet it is solely in virtue of this that I have succeeded in everything that I have done'.

In all his personal relations, self-interest inevitably stood foremost. 'I have always been the victim of my attachment to him,' declared Jean Lannes, and there was no one more devoted among all Napoleon's marshals, but: 'He only loves you by fits and starts: that is, when he has need of you.' This same rather unattractive quality manifested itself in Napoleon's associations with women, which played no small part in his life. 'Fortune,' he declared to Marmont, 'is a woman, and the more she does for me the more I will demand from her.'

His philosophy was essentially that the function of women should be confined to bed, family and Church; this was abundantly reflected in the *Code Civil*, which removed many of the rights of women. The aim of education must be 'not that girls should think, but that they should believe'. He complained: 'We Westerners have spoilt everything by treating women too well. We are quite wrong to make them almost our equals. The Eastern peoples have been much more sensible.'

As with his essential disinterest in *la bonne table*, as already noted, he endeavoured to keep his amorous affairs on a matter-of-fact basis. He was, however, by no means immune himself to passion in all its facets. There was hardly a woman in his entourage whom he did not attempt to seduce, and he could be relentless when rebuffed; as with the virtuous Mme Récamier, who preserved her virginity – it was alleged – even with her boring banker husband. Nor, much as he may have affected to despise women, could he ever entirely restrain his passions from spilling over into his professional life – notably, of course, where Josephine was concerned.

It is always something of a mystery how Napoleon and the Creole, conveniently widowed at the age of thirty-one by Robespierre, and ravishingly beautiful (despite her blackened stubs of teeth ruined by a childhood of chewing Martiniquais sugarcane) ever became destined for each other. There was no cogent reason for Barras, master of the Directoire, to hand over a perfectly good mistress to a relatively insignificant young general (although he appears to have persisted with certain rights for a few years afterwards); or for Josephine to marry an impecunious young officer. Napoleon deluded himself that she was wealthy enough to pay his debts and to provide him with heirs, on both of which counts he was disappointed. She also lied to him about her age. Wildly extravagant, Josephine in fact increased his indebtedness. Her purchasing of Malmaison for ff325,000 was an astronomic sum, which she had no means of paying.

The match began inauspiciously, with the future Emperor being bitten on the leg by Josephine's pug while making love to her on their wedding night, and little time elapsed before she was flagrantly unfaithful to him. He once declaimed haughtily, on the subject of separate bedrooms: 'Crimes only divide the husband from the wife ... only *one* for me and Madame Bonaparte.' Yet male fidelity was not rated quite so highly in the Corsican scale of things.

In Egypt, Napoleon in his separation was solaced by a lady called 'La Bellilote', who concealed a well-rounded pair of buttocks in tight officer's breeches, and there were a series of ladies like the beautiful young actress Mademoiselle George, whom, subsequently, Napoleon shared with his conqueror, Wellington. She indiscreetly and unfavourably observed, the Iron Duke was 'le plus fort' as a lover. But for most of his life it was Josephine who held some special magic for Napoleon. 'Sweet and matchless Josephine ... How strangely you work upon my heart!' he wrote in one of his many passionate letters to her; letters that all too often brought no reply. Abandoned for many months to her own company, creating the garden at Malmaison was not enough to keep the hot-blooded Creole occupied. Napoleon knew this and while campaigning in distant lands she was constantly in his mind, driving him on and plaguing him with doubts:

> I have not spent a day without loving you; I have not spent a
> night without embracing you; I have not so much as drunk a
> single cup of tea without cursing the pride and ambition which
> force me to remain separated from the moving spirit of my life.
> In the midst of my duties, whether I am at the head of my army
> or inspecting the camps, my beloved Josephine stands alone in
> my heart, occupies my mind, fills my thoughts...

Then there would come the inevitable note on professional matters: 'PS. The war this year has changed beyond recognition. I have meat, bread and fodder distributed ... My soldiers are showing inexpressible confidence in me; you alone are a source of chagrin to me; you alone are the joy and torment of my life.' A year later he would be writing, from Verona: 'I love you no longer; on the contrary, I detest you. You are a wretch, truly perverse ... You never write to me at all, you do not love your husband ... What business is so vital that it robs you of the time to write to your faithful lover?' A few days afterwards: 'I have defeated the enemy ... I am dead with exhaustion. I beg you leave with all speed for Verona; I need you ...'

Napoleon had few illusions: 'She wanted everything,' he once complained. Late in life he admitted to Bertrand, with what seems like more than passing honesty, 'I really did love her ... but had no respect for her ... She had the prettiest little —— imaginable.' Whatever that may have been, it was for many years to wield a powerful influence over the most powerful man in Europe, in peace as in war.

Indispensable as Josephine was in the rise of Napoleon's 'star', equally essential to him in all his endeavours at civic reform was the person of Jean Jacques Régis de Cambacérès. Aged forty-five when he became Second Consul in 1799, Cambacérès was a flamboyant homosexual and pretentious gourmet, though smart Parisians deemed his parties occasions to be avoided at all costs. He dressed like a peacock, provoking much derision on the streets of Paris, but he was also an outstanding jurist, an administrator and manipulator in the corridors of power. Among the many turncoats employed by Napoleon, he had once been chairman of the revolution's Committee of Public Safety. With a capacity for work rivalling even Napoleon's, as President of the Senate, the Council of Ministers, the Conseil d'État, the Conseil du Sceau des Titres and the Privy Council, there was scarcely any aspect of Napoleon's 'Peace Machine' that lay outside the ken of Cambacérès. Not empowered to take decisions himself, over the five years that Napoleon was absent from Paris during his fourteen and a half in power, Cambacérès faithfully drafted him a daily report. Unlike Fouché and Talleyrand, he was to remain totally loyal to his master, being created a Prince of the Empire and Duke of Parma for his pains.

Then there was Napoleon's Minister of Police, the thoroughly odious, unscrupulous but eminently efficient Joseph Fouché. Like Talleyrand, Fouché started life in the Church. Typically, although he had ruthlessly suppressed a revolt against Robespierre in Lyons, after the fall of Toulon in 1793 Fouché had gloated to a colleague in Paris, 'Tonight we will execute 1,213 insurgents. *Adieu* – tears of joy flow from my eyes.' His cruelty during the revolution had brought him spurious renown; during the massacres in Lyons he was alleged to have been seen carrying a pair of human ears dangling from either side of his cleric's hat. But when Thermidor arrived Fouché had acted with equal zeal against Robespierre and the Jacobins. Then, under the Directoire, he had worked as a spy for Barras in Holland.

Operating always like a mole, underground, Fouché was made Napoleon's dreaded Chief of Police after Brumaire, and stayed there for the next decade. In 1810, Napoleon sacked him for holding secret peace talks with the British. After the retreat from Moscow in 1812, Napoleon, no longer trusting him to remain behind in Paris working behind his back, dispatched Fouché first to Prussia, then as ruler to Illyria. But, unpleasant a human being as he was, Fouché was a born survivor – among other things, he boasted a card index of *Who's Who* in the Empire that was dangerously important to any ruler. Reinstated as Napoleon's police chief at the beginning of the Hundred Days, Fouché returned to Paris almost immediately after Napoleon's abdication in 1814, made his peace with Louis XVIII and became the second richest man in France, but he ended life as an unwanted wanderer in Austria – cuckolded by his 26-year-old wife.

Profoundly unattractive, Fouché's character was etched into his face. 'Only the red rims of his half-closed eyelids relieved the identical colour of skin, hair and eyes,' according to one contemporary. Yet he was said to be a kind father and devoted husband. The forerunner of twentieth-century police chiefs like Himmler and Beria, Fouché's attitude to humanity was simply expressed as 'remove from every citizen that which is not necessary'. He was certainly one of the most accomplished politicians of all time; Napoleon saw him and his ubiquitous intelligence service as 'living in everybody's boots', and in both his rise and his maintenance of power Fouché was essential to Napoleon.

Inevitably, one thinks in the same moment of Talleyrand, the greatest and the wiliest diplomat and politician of them all. He and Fouché were forever coupled by Chateaubriand's devastating remark, as the two entered the room, *bras dessus, bras dessous*, at the time of the Restoration: 'A vision of Vice supported by Crime.' One Scottish peer thought Talleyrand was 'the most disgusting individual I ever saw. His complexion is that of a corpse considerably advanced in corruption.' When death finally overtook him, Louis-Philippe's reaction to the news was: 'But there is no judging from appearances with Talleyrand!'

Like Fouché, Talleyrand was a Vicar of Bray of his times, serving all the rulers of France from the revolution to Louis Philippe with equal zeal. Charles Maurice de Talleyrand de Périgord, one time Bishop of Autun, but self-defrocked, he married and – doubtless chiefly on account of his devastating wit – was generally irresistible to women. His worldly and acquisitive tastes were highly developed. Mirabeau, never one to mince words, remarked that he 'would sell his soul for money; and he would be right, for he would be exchanging dung for gold'.

Talleyrand had escaped the Terror by fleeing to America as a royalist exile. There, working in a Philadelphia bookshop, his patron, Saint-Méry, as a sideline to books had introduced contraceptives to the grateful Americans. In his two years in America he mixed with a curious group of expatriate aristocrats, while shocking staid Philadelphians by consorting publicly with a lady of colour. He did, however, ingest the useful lesson that the young United States remained at heart still more English than not; therefore, in the event of renewed war with England, France would have to lean over backwards to prevent America falling into the enemy camp. It was against the background of such sensible advice that Napoleon was persuaded to make the Louisiana Purchase, thereby presenting Washington with the best bargain – at $15 million – in US history.

When appointed Minister of Foreign Affairs by the Directoire
on his return from America in 1797, Talleyrand was already
forty-three. He would serve France, and Napoleon, well for the
next ten years; then, after Tilsit – resigning in repugnance at
Napoleon's continued quest for world domination – would serve
his enemy, the Tsar of Russia with equal zeal. But, in the well-
chosen words of his biographer, Duff Cooper, the difference
between Talleyrand and Fouché was that for the former: 'politics
meant the settlement of dynastic or international problems
discussed in a ball-room or across the dinner-table; for Fouché
the same word meant street-corner assassination, planned by
masked conspirators in dark cellars'.

4   *In Pursuit of* La Gloire

I will surprise the world by the grandeur and rapidity of my strokes.
Napoleon to Cambacérès, August 1805

The year 1804 introduced the three years of Napoleon's greatest successes. They began that December with his coronation at Notre-Dame and ended with the triumphant conclusion of a victorious European peace on the raft at Tilsit. They incorporated his most brilliant military feats, Austerlitz and Jena. Unfortunately for him, however, neither was decisive, and 1804 was also accompanied by two dark shadows cast, first by a major reverse in strategic policy in failing with his invasion of England, and secondly – his worst crime – the wanton murder of the Duc d'Enghien. Both shadows, lengthening after Tilsit, would haunt him to the end.

Although the coronation and the creation of the Empire provided Napoleon with the semblance of legitimacy and continuity of succession, it did not bring peace. Alas for Napoleon's imperial grand design, and alas for Europe – in the words of Winston Churchill – 'the tourist season was short'. The Peace of Amiens was to turn out to be something like the Ribbentrop–Molotov non-aggression pact of 1939 – little more than a brief unnatural truce that both sides sought to vitiate, while laying the blame on the other.

Soon France and England were at war again. Already in the year preceding his coronation, once more abandoning Paris, Napoleon had begun amassing barges on the Channel coast with the intention of invading that implacable, relentless enemy – Pitt the Younger's England. In Boulogne, and on the Seine, there took place an extraordinary activity of shipyard building. The Esplanade of the Invalides was covered with sheds where hundreds of workers hammered away at the flotilla of flat-bottomed boats, while most of the left bank of the Seine became one vast naval shipyard. Napoleon himself was there, directing manœuvres and making a mock landing; England watched in alarm. Napoleon's strategy was to dispatch Admiral Villeneuve and his fleet on a feint to the West Indies, to appear to threaten British possessions there. Having led Nelson off on a wild-goose chase, Villeneuve was to double back with all speed to reappear in the Channel with a superior invasion force led by some sixty battleships. But Villeneuve and the French Navy, rickety as it was (not least through the loss of many of its best officers during the revolution), were beaten to the trick by a vigilant Nelson, after 14,000 miles of pursuit. Blocked from the Channel, Villeneuve headed south for Cadiz – and, eventually, Trafalgar. He had failed the new Emperor.

News of the invasion became muted; then, at the end of August 1805, with precipitate speed Napoleon switched plans, left the Camp of Boulogne, and marched eastwards. Word had reached him that the Austrians and Russians, backed by the hesitant Prussians, were combining forces to attack; but with incredible speed he struck out across Europe to forestall them. At every turn he outwitted and outfought the dazed Allies with their cumbersome armies – first at Ulm, then at Austerlitz in the middle of what is now the Czech Republic. Morale in the Grande Armée was never higher: every soldier was persuaded by his mesmeric leader that he did indeed carry a marshal's baton in his knapsack, and that, even if he died, his death would bring back *la gloire* for France. The risks for the Grande Armée, heavily outnumbered and far from its bases, were enormous, but at Austerlitz on 2 December Napoleon carried off his finest victory.

Though far from being a 'perfect' battle, Austerlitz was certainly one of history's most remarkable victories – decisive, at least temporarily – and it showed Napoleon's genius at its best. All depended on his extraordinary *coup d'œil* for topography, his instinctive understanding of what the enemy was going to do, and his ability to act with total decisiveness. Also he had an army in which he could place absolute confidence. For many days he had studied the terrain meticulously, observing that in late autumn the Moravian mist filled the hollows until – by mid-morning – the sun would break through to dispel it. Banking on this, he concealed Soult's chief assault force down in the valley; then, as anticipated, the sun arrived to reveal the enemy moving off the Pratzen Heights opposite, intending to take Napoleon's outnumbered army from the flank. Instead he hit them by surprise from their most vulnerable quarter, rolling up the whole Austro-Russian force in a battle of annihilation by the end of the day.

As well as its adoption as a moral, and cultural symbol, the *beau soleil d'Austerlitz* became a touchstone of the Emperor's invincibility, indeed of the whole Napoleonic legend. Unfortunately, it was also to prove almost too complete a victory, going to Napoleon's head and establishing copybook tactics that he would re-employ again and again – until, at last, the Allies would turn them against him.

From Austerlitz the Grand Armée headed north, still further into the dangerous depths of Europe, to crush the recalcitrant Prussians at Jena and Auerstädt the following year. But, as with most dictators, these triumphs would also mean that Napoleon had to keep on going, producing one triumph after another abroad. As Wellington once remarked of him, Napoleon was like a cannonball – he had to keep in motion; the moment he ceased it was all over. The pursuit of *la gloire* and triumph led him into Poland, in pursuit of the not-quite-defeated Russians, masters in the art of fighting withdrawals, and into the arms of Marie Walewska in Warsaw. The campaigns of 1805–7, Napoleon's most triumphant, ended with the bloody battles of Eylau and Friedland in distant East Prussia. Had he but realised it, those two battles were harbingers of the future; the 'glory days' were over. What looked like a decisive, definitive conclusion came with the Peace of Tilsit, signed on a raft midstream on the River Niemen, the very frontier of Russia, between Napoleon and all the rulers of continental Europe, whose armies he had defeated one after the other.

It was indeed a historic, head-turning moment. Yet one nation was absent among the defeated negotiators, and uncowed – England. Just as Napoleon had been trouncing his land-borne enemies at Austerlitz, so unseen, far to his rear, Nelson and his 'distant, storm-beaten ships, upon which the Grand Army never looked' (in the oft-repeated words of American historian, Admiral Mahan), were winning at Trafalgar the sea-battle that eventually would lead to the destruction of all Napoleon's imperial hopes.

Domestically, the disaster at Trafalgar was effectively obscured by the triumphant sequence of news from eastern Europe – and by ongoing economic crisis at home. In fact, the victories of the Grande Armée had come only just in time to halt, and reverse, a major domestic disaster.

From the earliest days of the Consulate, the shaky French economic and financial system – ruined by the revolution – had also received the full benefit of the three Consuls' attention, accompanied with often draconian measures. Already under the corrupt Directoire, taxation had been thoroughly overhauled, with taxes restructured and – for almost the first time – actually collected with ruthless efficiency. The Banque de France was established in 1800, and granted total control over the national debt and the issue of paper money. Industrial prosperity was stimulated by ubiquitous government intervention, and various innovations of social welfare were encouraged, though along largely paternalistic lines.

Nevertheless, trade unions were ruthlessly stamped on as 'Jacobin' institutions, or as diseases exported by the insidious British. Unemployment was kept at a low level, but labour was hard and the hours long. In summer, builders worked from 6 a.m. to 7 p.m.; the life expectancy of bakers was under fifty; and up to 1813, children under ten were still employed in the mines. From 1803 onwards every working man had to carry a registration book stamped by his employer, without which he was treated as a vagabond. When it came to litigation it was always the employer's word that was accepted. In rural France, the life of the average peasant – though improved by the revolutionary land settlement – was not much affected by either the Consulate or the Empire. The great roads built by Napoleon radiated out towards frontiers with distinct military purposes, but did little to bring the countryside into contact with the modern world.

Generally speaking, however, both peasant and urban working classes seem to have been better fed than they were either before 1789 or, indeed, after 1815, partly because of strict government controls placed on corn exports and price levels, and they came to regard the Napoleonic era as one of relative prosperity. Napoleon claimed to have gained the allegiance of the working classes by 'bread and circuses', and certainly the appeal to native jingoism of great victories such as Marengo, and then Austerlitz, went far to mitigate discontent arising from any loss of civil or political liberties.

On the other hand, further up the social scale there were great – and often scandalous – opportunities for self-enrichment. Typical of both the regime and the man, Talleyrand, having negotiated the Peace of Lunéville (which, in 1801, had brought to an end the War of the Second Coalition with Austria), made a fortune by buying up Austrian bonds issued in Belgium. He knew that one of the stipulations of the treaty was that these bonds were subsequently to he honoured. Was there ever a worse case of 'insider-trading'? Meanwhile, by 1804 the bourgeoisie owned approximately twice as much land in parts of northern France as it had done in 1789.

For a while, even after the Peace of Amiens ended, the boom in trade continued. Proclamation of the Empire brought about great activity in trading luxuries, and with it prosperity in France free-wheeled for another couple of years. Then the French economy plummeted. A poor harvest made bread prices soar, and finances were in a mess with the budget showing an immense deficit. Huge manufacturing stocks piled up. There was serious unemployment, which recruitment for the Grande Armée only partially sopped up, with the remainder of the unemployed being set to work on Napoleon's new construction work in Paris. National bankruptcy loomed. Paying for the new war resulted in a heavy increase in taxation, which in turn provoked something akin to panic on the Bourse. Thus it became absolutely imperative for Napoleon to win a swift and decisive victory; otherwise the country would be in serious danger of bankruptcy. Then, in the autumn of 1805 – just as Napoleon stood on the threshold of his greatest military successes – Paris was rocked by the collapse of the highly respectable Banque Récamier. The bank had actually suspended withdrawals, thereby resulting in a sequence of bankruptcies and industries brought to a standstill.

The shock of the Banque Récamier failure hit Paris like a thunderbolt. The bank was a rock-like institution; the elderly Jacques Récamier a tower of respectability; his wife, Juliette, renowned for her salon in the Chaussée d'Antin (pointedly, it had once been the home of Louis XVI's last Minister of Finance), almost a paragon of virtue. With mischievous intent, the journalist Joseph Fiévée (who had it in for Récamier) wrote:

> The bankruptcy of Monsieur Récamier is without argument the most scandalous thing that one has seen for a long time, and although the police may have forced all the journals to present it

in an interesting and sentimental manner, one will never be able
to persuade the public that a dealer in money doing his job could
let 19 millions go missing.

It all has a ring about it that twenty-first-century New Yorkers
might recognise.

In fact, however, although the Minister of the Treasury
himself was under suspicion of embezzlement, and the wily
Talleyrand too freely boasted of having made a killing from
insider-trading: 'I bought stock on 17th in Brumaire, and I sold
it again on the 19th' (it being recalled that Napoleon seized
power on 18 Brumaire), the Récamiers seem to have behaved
impeccably in the wake of disaster. Juliette rejected all 'lucrative
and culpable subterfuges' – a display of integrity unusual in
Paris of the early Empire.

Yet when Récamier pleaded for a modest government loan to
bail out the bank, Napoleon was unapproachable and unfor-
giving, writing from Austerlitz within days of his triumph (7
December 1805): 'Is it at a time like this that I must be obliged
to make advances to men who have got themselves involved in
bad businesses?' and, more brutally: 'I am not the lover of
Madame Récamier, not I, and I am not going to come to the
help of *négociants* who keep up a house costing 600,000 francs
a year.' An Italian diplomat wrote: 'In the middle of due admir-
ation aroused by Bonaparte's astonishing campaign, the nation's
credit, undermined everywhere, threatens ruin everywhere.'
Indeed, it was almost certainly only by the success of Napoleon's
triumphs on distant battlefields like Austerlitz and Jena that
Paris escaped serious disorders.

Then, after Austerlitz, miraculously the economy appeared
to recover – at least temporarily – with government bonds rising
dizzily from 45 per cent to 66 per cent.

The momentary ripples of excitement set up by news of the

Grande Armée's entry into Vienna in the autumn of 1805 swiftly subsided, while tidings that followed in a few weeks of the great victory at Austerlitz evoked hardly more of a public reaction. Seen from the street, history in the making looked rather less rosy than it had done following Marengo. A confidant of Napoleon, the journalist Joseph Fiévée, wrote to him: 'the morning after, everyone was talking about his less than brilliant personal affairs, about the scarcity of money, about the excessive interest imposed, and the nullity of commercial operations'. There was little interest whipped up even by the display in the streets of Paris of captured enemy flags and war booty. Wrote Fiévée: 'A proportion of the people had so evidently been paid [to cheer], that public decency was affronted.' When Napoleon returned from Austerlitz on 26 January 1806, he was sorely disappointed by the apathy he found in Paris. The ever unctuous Cambacérès declared, 'The joy of the people resembled intoxication', but this may have been at best a modest exaggeration. In fact everything rather suggested a populace distracted by its own problems nearer home.

The winter of 1806-7 was one of difficulty and hardship as the English naval blockade hit not only Paris but cities as far away as Lyons. Then, on 27 July 1807, cannon thundering out from the Invalides announced that the Emperor had returned from the east and the triumphal peace imposed at Tilsit. He had been absent for a total of 306 days – the longest he would ever be away from the capital. To commemorate the Grande Armée's breath-taking military triumphs, but also in keeping with populist methods, Napoleon ordered Paris to be thrown into a frenzy of celebration. Military bands and spectators jammed the avenues, as the magnificent Imperial Guard made its triumphal entry. There were endless parades, balls and fêtes. Wine flowed throughout the twelve *arrondissements*, while the Paris 'Vaudeville' put on a show appropriately entitled *Ils arrivent*. Heady stuff! And a superb recompense for the Grande Armée, which had marched to the Niemen and back. As always, Napoleon knew precisely how to assure himself of the loyalty of his soldiers. The following day another extravagant fête was thrown by the Senate at the Luxembourg; alas – perhaps an augury of the gods – pelting icy rain and hail turned the occasion into a rout.

The only thing missing from the festivities was the Emperor himself, who, on the appointed day, eternally restless, had already set off again on his voyages. Perhaps the most brilliant of all the celebrations that followed Tilsit was that marking the Emperor's birthday on 15 August. Fouché went over the top, and declared in a note addressed to the Emperor that 'Today's *fête* is really national. Foreigners have been able to compare the birthday of Napoleon to that of Saint-Louis ...' Meanwhile the regime's mythologists, supported by the papal legate, came up with the helpful discovery that, at the time of Diocletian, there had been an early Neapolitan martyr called Saint Napoleon. Henceforth 15 August – convenient for the adherence of the *bien-pensants* in that it was also the date of the ratification of the Concordat with Rome – was to become a kind of saint's day in the Napoleonic calendar, far eclipsing the revolutionary *Quatorze Juillet*, to which the Emperor paid only minimal lip service.

Hubris, the device that destroyed the Greek heroes of ancient mythology – was it now to be the undoing of Napoleon? Emulating Louis XIV after the Peace of Nijmegen in 1678, the Emperor now bestowed upon himself the title *le Grand*. Indeed, he gazed down on an empire that stretched from the Pyrenees to the Niemen, ruled over either by puppet sovereigns or by members of his clan promoted to unimaginable heights; an empire far greater than anything achieved by Louis XIV, greater (at least, in appearance) even than the world of Charlemagne. Ruling a France intoxicated with glory, after Tilsit the Emperor was no longer in a mood to listen to anybody. He closed down the Tribunate and, on Talleyrand's resignation, replaced him by the docile, sycophantic Minister of the Interior, Champagny. Among other changes, a more rigorous court etiquette kept everyone literally at arm's length, unable to approach him without the approval of Duroc, Grand Marshal of the Palace. Thus Napoleon became surrounded by sycophants, a sure sign of the corruption of power.

The Peace of Tilsit seemed to give him endless options. But would he take them? Would the peace last, any more than the Peace of Amiens had? Older Frenchmen wondered where it would all end – not only Talleyrand. For he, foreseeing what lay ahead, resigned in despair, to offer his services to Napoleon's enemy, the Tsar. Within barely a year, intuition dictated that general war was going to begin again. Napoleon got himself involved in Iberia, where eventually the 'Spanish Ulcer' would bring him down. Paris would witness no more triumphal entries quite like Tilsit. But, at least on the economic level, it had restored to France a mirror-image of prosperity, with Napoleon promising to set aside for a whole year half a million francs a month to keep the factories going.

Yet Tilsit had won Napoleon no real friends in Europe. It had presented him with every scrap of power he could possibly need, but in the character of the man on whom all depended, there had been a worrying transformation. Talleyrand found that he was 'intoxicated by himself'; even his voice sounded different. Mme de Rémusat observed of him that 'his despotism increased daily', and with it his passion for power – which was now total. Meanwhile, from his far-flung army HQs in eastern Europe, he had never ceased to bombard the administration in Paris with plans for civil innovations. Although under Napoleon France was more centralised upon Paris – the symbol and focus of his *gloire* – than it ever had been, and every act of the Napoleonic drama was played out there, when he was away at the wars it sometimes seemed that the capital had been reduced to no more than an out-station of his *Quartier Général*. From his Finkenstein HQ in East Prussia a thousand miles away, he had managed amazingly during the past year to run his empire of 70 million people, involving himself in almost every facet of life. He had sent off no fewer than 300 bullying, chivvying and commanding letters in the spring of 1807 alone. It was as a dictator that France now began to see him, and no one could say 'no' to his plethora of edicts.

5 *The Master Builder*

> If I were the master of France, I would like to make Paris not only
> the most beautiful city in the world, the most beautiful that ever
> existed, but also the most beautiful that could ever exist ... If the
> Heavens had granted me another twenty years and some leisure, you
> would have looked in vain for the Old Paris; you would not have
> been able to see the slightest trace of it ...
>
> **Napoleon in 1798**

Between the peaces of Amiens and Tilsit was the period when
Napoleon dedicated himself to his plans for making Paris 'the
most beautiful city that could ever exist'. From Tilsit, after
settling the destiny of Europe, he sent a warning note to his
Minister of the Interior, Champagny: '*Monsieur le Ministre*,
peace has been made with the foreigners; now I am going to
make war on your offices ...' He was swift to carry out his
threat, sweeping away the inefficient city administration that
he had inherited from the Directoire, with its system of incompetent elected bodies. Under the Empire its capital would now
be run by various *conseils d'administration*. These were
endowed with immense powers; presided over by Napoleon
himself, all were answerable to the Minister of the Interior, who
in turn represented the full authority of the Emperor. In many
ways there was a resemblance to the system under the *ancien
régime* whereby the Prefect of the Seine filled the function of
the former Prévot des Marchands and the Prefect of Police
shadowed that of the Lieutenant Général. It was turning the
clock back to 1789 – except that Napoleon carried with him far
more power than Louis XVI, or even *le grand Louis*. Most
important of all was the special body set up to coordinate the
efforts of administrators, architects and engineers instructed to

carry out Napoleon's building plans. Though he endeavoured to run the city like an army, it was not the kind of army to which he was accustomed – or that would bend to his every whim. Of the opposition he met when trying to reform the anarchic Halles in 1810, his criticism was typical: 'I don't like this mess ... there is no discipline here.'

Despite the formidable powers of the bureaucracy that Napoleon set up in Paris, however, one of the extraordinary features of his regime is that this highly centralised and increasingly autocratic state was in fact run from the inside of a tent, or from some Polish château – or from wherever Napoleon happened to be. Ministers affected to see largely the grandiose and theatrical side of this inconvenient arrangement: 'Your Majesty has so well accustomed us to have recourse to his sagacity for the smallest details,' declared the sycophantic Jean Baptiste de Nomprère de Champagny, promoted from an inconsequential but doggedly loyal clerk in the Ministry of the Interior to succeed Talleyrand on his resignation, 'that, always governed by his spirit as by his decrees, we forget that he is 600 leagues from us, in the middle of his armies, having in front of him the reunited forces of the most powerful empire of the world, protecting the south and the east of Europe.' It was hardly the language of a Colbert speaking to a Louis XIV. Up to his return in July 1807, over the three campaigns of 1805–7 Napoleon was out of Paris for most of the year – he would never stay away so long again. And in spirit, he had never left; whether ordaining the administration of Paris, and its building, or running the country, fundamentally the government of France was where Napoleon was – Vienna, Berlin, Warsaw, Finkenstein, Tilsit.

Every day his minions in Paris would be bombarded by letters, orders and draft decrees. One of Napoleon's most remarkable contributions lay in the streamlining of communications and post – especially anything radiating out of his own headquarters, wherever it might be on the continent of Europe. He (and, indeed, Josephine) would think little of making a 300-mile trip by bumpy carriage, and the speed with which his system of couriers could relay messages was quite phenomenal. As an essential aid to morale, every effort was made for soldiers serving with the Grande Armée to send and receive home mail, while the sheer scale of Napoleon's own correspondence is staggering. He must have been the most hands-on leader the world has ever known. Winston Churchill would bombard generals and civil servants alike with his 'Pray tell . . .' memoranda all through the Second World War – but only concerning the conduct of the war and never on a scale comparable to the French dictator. And, because of the totality of power he had concentrated in himself, Napoleon could be assured that toadies all the way down the line would tumble over themselves to do his bidding.

In the midst of planning the most brilliant battle, when not ordering up III Corps from Vienna, or instructing Murat how to deploy at Friedland, there was no single element of life in which Napoleon's barrage of letters would not intervene – some might call it 'meddle'. From Poland in December 1806, he would write to Champagny: 'My intention is to construct a Bourse which would relate to the grandeur of the capital . . . propose to me a convenient locality. It has to be vast, in order to have promenades around it. I would like an isolated place.' The same month, to mark the battle of Austerlitz, a decree signed in Posen called for the Madeleine to be transformed into a *temple de la gloire* for the Grand Armée, bearing on its façade the words: 'L'empereur Napoleon aux soldats de la Grande-Armée.' Later, while in East Prussia preparing for the bitter Friedland campaign, an angry letter flew off to Fouché: 'I understand that the city of Paris is no longer illuminated . . . those in charge are scoundrels.'

From Tilsit, a thousand miles away, he would be fretting that the fountains in Paris weren't working properly, or that the Ourcq Canal was not completed; or he would be decreeing demolition of the old houses on the Saint-Michel bridge. The following year, on his way to Spain, he would write to an *haut fonctionnaire* in Paris:

> Monsieur Cretet, make me a little report on the work that I have ordered. Where is the Bourse? Is the Convent of the Filles Saint-Thomas demolished? Is the building rising? What has been done at the Arc de Triomphe? ... Shall I pass over the Pont d'Iéna on my return? So much for Paris...

'Poor *fonctionnaires* – poor architects!' one sighs; and perhaps poor Paris! A year later, 1809, to Fouché from Schönbrunn after the Battle of Wagram: 'If you have any intimation that the engineer in charge of paving in Paris is a thief, have him arrested at once.'

It was not just the sticks and stones of Paris that would draw Napoleon's attention from afar. As will be seen shortly, the Paris theatre in particular would feel the full thrust of his attention. The Bonaparte family, too, regularly bore the brunt of Napoleon's incessant instructions and memos; among the hundreds of letters dispatched from Tilsit in the spring of 1807, one on 4 April castigated his brother Louis, now King of Holland: 'You govern your nation like a docile, timorous monk ... A king issues orders and does not beg. You had better apply those paternalistic, effeminate traits you display in governing your country to your domestic life ...' On 16 May, he would tell his brother Jérôme, who was suffering from piles: 'The best way to make them disappear is to apply leeches.' His troublesome critic, Mme de Staël, also had to be dealt with; on 20 April: 'I am writing to the Minister of Police [Fouché] on the subject of that foolish woman, Madame de Staël ... She is to remain in Geneva ...' On 6 May, like a late-twentieth-century Eurocrat, he would ordain: 'I want the whole of Europe to have one currency; it will make trading much easier.'

*

It was in rebuilding the central area of Paris, so worked over by previous rulers in past centuries, that Napoleon particularly was to leave his mark. To achieve this he resorted to draconian measures (as only he could) to take over property. Convents left ravaged by the revolution were especially vulnerable. Property owners were driven out with little recompense. Creating the new Rue Castiglione, for instance, required demolition of the ancient Feuillant convent; disappeared also was the historic Salle de Manège, where abolition of the monarchy had been proclaimed. Later on, in his grandiose plans of the palace at Chaillot for his infant son, the King of Rome, he discovered that the land there belonged to a former secretary in the cabinet, Philippe Nettement. The unhappy Nettement was told forthwith that he had to sell; his architect estimated the value at over ff500,000, but – bullied and even threatened with eviction by the police – Nettement had to settle for a price one-third of its value.

Remorselessly, Napoleon would raze (in 1808) medieval gems like the church of Saint André, where Voltaire was baptised, and whose Gothic tower had for centuries dominated its *quartier* on the Left Bank. Often Napoleon would obtain allies in the newspapers of the day, which, disinterested in the past, managed to find excellent reasons for justifying his demolitions.

We have already seen how, impelled by the catastrophic floods of 1801–2, Napoleon had begun his building works with his reconstruction of the *quais* and bridges of the Seine, and the extensive list of streets and buildings already targeted by him when First Consul. The bomb blast that had come so close to assassinating him on Christmas Eve 1800 gave Napoleon a good pretext such as his predecessors – notably Louis XIV – had lacked for clearing the medieval slum areas cluttering up the approaches to the Tuileries and the Louvre. He started by briskly demolishing the forty-odd houses damaged by the explosion.

Vanished for ever was the Rue Niçaise, where the bomb had exploded. Now re-christened the Musée Napoléon, at the suggestion of the obsequious Cambacérès, the Louvre was completed in 1803 to house the treasures that had flowed from his recent campaigns. In the cleared area alongside his new Rue de Rivoli, Napoleon laid down the stately north wing of the Louvre, but – like so much else – that too had to await completion at the hands his nephew, Napoleon III.

One of the objectives in clearing out the old buildings was his desire, as he admitted to Cretet in 1808, to be able to see the whole of the Louvre from his balcony. At the other end, facing Louis XIV's great portico, the ancient Saint-Germain l'Auxerrois, which had survived Louis XIV's ambitions, only narrowly escaped being transformed into a monumental church – to be named after the mythical 'Saint Napoleon'. In preserving intact the old, historic sections of François Premier's and Louis XIV's Louvre, Napoleon fortunately resisted the impulses of his architects, showing remarkably good architectural sense in his instructions to Champagny: 'One must leave to each of the sections the character of its century, while adopting for the new work a more economic style.' Most important was the establishment there, from 1803 onwards, of Europe's most immense art gallery, to provide a permanent home for the vast treasure-trove of works of art that he had looted – first from Italy, then from the other conquered and occupied countries.

As a director to run the new Musée Napoleon for him, the Emperor chose one of those extraordinary geniuses produced by an extraordinary age – Vivant Denon. A former diplomat, *chargé d'affaires* in Naples, Denon was already fifty-five when appointed in 1802. 'Citizen' Denon, who in paintings looked like the neat, tidy-minded clerk that he indeed was, was also something of a *roué* (an attribute that quite appealed to Napoleon) as well as being an accomplished artist in his own right. He had travelled with Napoleon on the abortive Egyptian expedition of 1798, to return with a remarkable portfolio of sketches. Thereafter he accompanied Napoleon on almost all his campaigns, becoming known as *l'œil de l'armée*.

The idea of a gallery accessible to the public originated with the much-maligned Louis XVI, when Marigny, brother of Mme de Pompadour, had opened the royal galleries that had previously been kept as the private preserve of the monarchy. It had been Louis XVI's notion of reuniting everything that the crown possessed of 'beauty in painting and sculpture' under the name of 'museum' (a concept imitated from England). The Directoire resumed and embellished the theme: 'The time has arrived where the reign [of the fine arts] must pass to France to confirm and embellish that of liberty' it was declared.

Between them, Napoleon and Denon were absolutely clear as to what they intended in the name of French culture. Explained Denon, 'The French Republic by its force, the superiority of its light and its artists, is the only country in the world which could provide an inviolable asylum for these masterpieces.' (Here was a masterly argument for the British Museum to follow in its consistent refusal to hand back the Elgin Marbles to a polluted, earthquake-prone Athens!) Napoleon followed this up by telling the Directoire as early as February 1797, 'We shall have everything that is beautiful in Italy, excepting a small number of objects which are to be found in Turin and Naples.'

Already the annexation of Belgium had brought to Paris a treasure trove of Rubens and Van Eycks. Then, for the opening of the magnificent 'Italian Gallery' on 14 July 1801, came Veronese's vast *Marriage of Cana*, brought from Venice – cut in two pieces, so as to be transported in an oxen cart. Seeing it for the first time, an English woman visitor to Paris during the peace was heard to exclaim: 'What a gallery, but what a gallery ... such as the world has never seen, in the way of grandeur and decorations.'

As in the theatre, Napoleon paid great interest – amounting to interference – in the museum that had been named after him. On his return from Jena, in September 1806, he was already complaining about the queues on a Saturday afternoon. As a result, opening hours were immediately extended on Saturdays and Sundays. Napoleon was also horrified to see the galleries equipped with smoking stoves, to keep the wretched *gardiens* warm: 'Get them out ... they will end up by burning my conquests!'

On every one of Napoleon's campaigns following Egypt, Denon was to be found busily sketching battlefields and soldiery for the glorification of the regime. But he was also tireless in seeking out and cataloguing artefacts for transportation to Paris, his principal commission, with total indifference to the humiliation of the subject nations that were being robbed. (As far as France herself was concerned, Napoleon showed some conscience, issuing, in May 1806, orders for the return of all religious paintings in his possession to the churches ransacked by the revolutionaries.) The Grande Armée nicknamed Denon the *huissier priseur* (hardly translatable: perhaps a 'confiscating bailiff'); he was in fact a looter on a scale that makes Hermann Goering look like something of an amateur. Under him, Napoleon's Paris, the new Rome, swiftly became the greatest art metropolis the world had ever seen – a reputation that would, remarkably, survive the ephemeral life of Napoleon's military conquests. What Denon collected still constitutes the nucleus of the Louvre's fourteenth-century gallery, and it is therefore perhaps not inappropriate that one of its principal wings continues to bear his name today.

Perhaps the most daring and visionary – and, indeed, one of the most lasting – of Napoleon's *embellissements* was his new Rue de Rivoli, carved out of the huddle of medieval buildings he

had destroyed between the Tuileries and the Louvre. It linked
Gabriel's classical Place de la Concorde, built under Louis XV,
with the Louvre and the Hôtel de Ville to the east; and, had
Napoleon survived to achieve his dreams, it would have continued all the way to the Porte Saint-Antoine. A remarkable
unitary triumph. As it was, it was to become the second longest
street in Paris, and one of the straightest. Designed by Napoleon's two favourite artists, Charles Percier and Pierre Fontaine,
it represented the most imposing achievement in large-scale
domestic housing since Henri IV's Place Dauphine at the
western tip of the Île de la Cité.

Strictest conditions were imposed on the new units; residents
were not to use hammers; there were to be no butchers or
bakers, or anybody using an oven. Perhaps as a result of these
restrictions, by 1810 so few houses had been built that Napoleon
was forced to grant special tax exemptions for twenty years to
developers, extended the following year to thirty. In contrast to
London, where inhabitants lived vertically in separate houses,
under Napoleon Parisians had taken to living horizontally, in
apartments – which helped his original grand design. The
seemingly endless perspective of the massive arcades and the
uninterrupted line of iron-work balconies above them today
still presents an effect unrivalled anywhere else in the world,
the true *grandeur* of Paris. The only part actually completed,
however (and that only partially), in Napoleon's day was the
grandly arcaded section facing the Louvre. Napoleon, though,
would doubtless be appalled at the rubbishy tourist traps that
have taken root today under Percier and Fontaine's magnificent
arcade.

Immediately on his return from Tilsit, Napoleon set to pestering
his officials again about the fountains of Paris; two years later,
shortly after Wagram, he was bullying the Ministry of the
Interior with regard to three fountains in the Faubourgs of

Saint-Denis and Saint-Martin. Here the water supply had been interrupted. But fountains were only part of the solution; where was the water to come from? Napoleon was obsessed by the water of Paris, and everything to do with it. With reason; ever since the days of King Philippe-Auguste in the twelfth and thirteenth centuries, administrators of Paris had been plagued by the problems of a safe, clean and abundant water supply, and with it the concomitant nightmares of mud and disease. The Seine, still encumbered with floating mills, boat wash-houses, abattoirs and tanneries, was polluted beyond belief. Most houses got their water from so-called purifying fountains, while the price of two pails of water, totalling three gallons, was two sous – a high price for the less affluent.

Neither the revolution nor the Directoire had done anything to improve matters; the basic, age-old squalor had only multiplied. Even by the end of the First Empire – in sharp contrast to London – many streets boasted no pavements, a danger to the lives of pedestrians, and not least to their clothing. With no proper sewage system, ordure still flowed down open sewers in the centre of the road; the *décrotteurs* provided an essential industry, scraping the thick, glutinous mud off the boots of passers-by. (And, to make matters worse, there was always a shortage of available public transport.) As it would on the way to and from Moscow, mud in Paris came close to defeating the all-powerful Emperor. Like the filth itself, Voltaire's famous remark that 'Paris was built like Nebuchadnezzar's statue – of gold and mud' still stuck.

Throughout history the sacred river of Paris had had an inconvenient habit of overflowing its banks at unpredictable intervals. The *inondation* of 1801–2, the worst since 1740, flooded cellars, cut the whole length of the Cours-de-le-Reine, and even reached certain points of the Rue Faubourg Saint-Honoré. Boats had to be used for transportation on a number of streets bordering the Seine. In 1806 Napoleon sent a decree from Warsaw ordering a new bridge to be called Pont d'Iéna – in honour of the battle.

Prior to the Empire, Paris had suffered from a serious shortage of bridges across the Seine. Little ferries used to ply back and forth even from the Louvre; thus, under Napoleon four new bridges were planned. All were to be toll bridges: 5 centimes for people on foot, 10 for horseback, 15 for a coach with one horse, 20 for a coach with two horses – and 2 centimes for a donkey. Napoleon even proposed a plan for a further, magnificent bridge – if he won at Waterloo. In fact, only two bridges were built and those with private money – the Pont d'Austerlitz being the last to be completed. At the same time, a scheme of January 1810 to place athwart the bridges eight colossal statues of his generals, *morts au champs d'honneur*, was never to reach fruition.

But one of Napoleon's most lasting achievements for Paris – and certainly the one for which the city remains most indebted – was to bring it fresh water all the way from the River Ourcq, via a 60-mile-long canal. This was to cost the immense sum of 38 million francs. By 1802 his work-force had already started digging the canal, partly as a solution to unemployment in the economic crisis. It was supposed to be completed by the autumn of 1805, but there were repeated delays. They drove Napoleon into a frenzy of impatience, though it was partly his fault, due to the shortage of manpower caused by the insatiable demands of his Grande Armée. Finally, on 2 December 1808 – the anniversary of Austerlitz, of course – a momentous opening ceremony announced the arrival of the sweet waters of the Ourcq in the Bassin de la Villette. Some Parisians, however, saw it as a possible danger to morality: 'An abundance of water at first encouraged the use, then the misuse, of the baths in Rome,' intoned one critic, Petit-Radel. 'Won't the ease of having water in one's own home lead to the same moral decay, once this oriental luxury is developed?' The bath-tub was long not considered a necessity of Parisian life; a *bidet* would suffice.

In the space gained by his demolitions round the Place du Carrousel, so named because it was the site where a young Louis XIV had held his magnificent extravaganza in 1662 to celebrate the birth of his heir, Napoleon planted a triumphal arch to commemorate Austerlitz. Compared with the Louvre behind it, some critics find the Carrousel a puny, even fussy affair. Certainly, as a project to which Napoleon had deep personal commitment (that and the Vendôme Column, also designed to commemorate the Austerlitz victory, were the only two actually completed during the Empire), the Carrousel attracted all the hands-on fussiness that was his prerogative. Its *pièce de résistance* comprised the famous horses looted from Venice by Napoleon during the first Italian campaign, which were to have a travel-worn career. Originally destined for a temple in ancient Corinth, they had already graced the arches of conquering emperors, Nero and Trajan, in Rome; they were transported to Constantinople by Theodosius, then brought back in the fourth crusade by the Venetians, and installed by Doge Dandolo high above St Mark's.

Remarkably, the Carrousel had its first stone laid only eight months after the battle of Austerlitz; then remained clad in scaffolding for the next two years. Napoleon was furious at the delay, demanding of the *intendant-général* when the scaffolding was finally to be removed. The answer came, 'We are only waiting for the statue of Your Majesty.' Napoleon flew into one of his terrifying rages: 'What statue are you talking about? – I never asked for one; nor did I order that my statue should be the principal subject of a monument raised by me and at my expense for the glory of the army which I had the honour to command.' He insisted that the chariot drawn by the four

Venetian horses remain empty. And so it did – until Waterloo, when the original horses were dispatched back to Venice, and an allegorical figure representing the Restoration filled the empty chariot, as it does today.

The Carrousel arch was, however, not enough to satisfy the Emperor at his peak of *la gloire*. A much more imposing monument atop the hill at the Étoile was projected, which – for all time – was to remain the single most dominating symbol of Paris. To grab his attention for the project, architect Fontaine assured Napoleon that the Étoile was 'in such an elevated situation that it would necessitate a monument of colossal grandeur'. Designed once again to immortalise Napoleon's martial successes, the history of the Arc de Triomphe was to be a turbulent one, and beyond even the all-powerful Napoleon's capacity to achieve. One of his first unrealised fantasies for the Étoile took the shape of a monster elephant, forty feet high. What it represented – whether a symbol of power, or Napoleon's covetous notions about India – no one quite seems to have known. Later the plan was to transfer it instead to the Place de la Bastille, where it would be cast, in 1811, in bronze from cannons captured from Spanish insurgents. But the disastrous Iberian adventure failed to supply enough captured weapons to build an elephant on such a scale, so instead it was fashioned out of wood and painted plaster. Under the Parisian weather the elephant gradually disintegrated, becoming the home of thousands of rats and somehow symbolic of the decay of empire.

So instead of a monster elephant at the Etoile came a monster arch. Designed by Jean Chalgrin, its first stones were laid in August 1806, just before Napoleon set off for the Jena campaign, but such was the immensity of the structure's predicted weight that foundations eight metres deep had to be dug. It had barely risen above ground level when, on 2 April 1810, Napoleon required a triumphal arch through which he could ride with his new Empress, Marie-Louise of Austria (Josephine having been divorced). In exasperation, he ordered up a full-scale moquette in wood and painted canvas; to complete it on time, all available carpenters were offered six times their normal wages in over-time, but in the end were commandeered by the Prefect of Police and paid no more than the normal rate. The effect of the gigantic mock-up was described as *saisissant*; it reflected both the best and the worst of Napoleon's personal rule. (The supreme irony was that, following completion of the Arc, the first triumphal procession to pass under consisted of Bismarck's Prussians fol-lowing the defeat of Napoleon's nephew, Napoleon III, in 1871.) Already in 1806 Napoleon would admit that the Arc 'would be a futile work which would have no kind of significance, if it wasn't a means of encouraging architecture'. (Also, he added: 'one mustn't lose any opportunity of humiliating the Russians and the English'.) Then the architect, Chalgrin, died in 1811 when the Arc had only reached a height of 5.4 metres, or just over one-tenth of its eventual height.

Typically, Napoleon lost interest – his restless mind now preoccupied with building a Louvre-sized palace for his infant son, the King of Rome.

Of all Napoleon's grandiose projects – like those of Louis XIV before him – dedicated to the pursuit of that illusive commodity so precious to French hearts, *la gloire*, the most imposing of all was the great imperial palace at Chaillot intended for the infant King of Rome, born in March 1811. Also designed to be a permanent monument to the power of Napoleonic Empire, the site selected stood on the Trocadero heights, where the present hideous 1930s Chaillot complex stands, facing the Eiffel Tower. It was then an idyllic corner of cottages and vineyards, where Catherine de Medici once had a country house, and where George Sand had happy childhood memories of 'warmth and gaiety' and recalled crying out 'Vive l'Empereur!' It was to be an 'Imperial city', 'a Kremlin a hundred times more beautiful than Moscow's', and larger even than decaying Versailles.

The idea was apparently generated by the court painter, David, remarking to the architect, Fontaine, what a fabulous site for a princely palace Chaillot could provide. Napoleon readily bought the idea; 20 million francs were set aside for the project, and with his usual dispatch he had work begin in May 1811 on what the architects, Fontaine and Percier, regarded as 'the vastest and most extraordinary work of our century' – a palace and a park covering the whole area of today's Trocadéro, la Muette and Porte Maillot, or about half the present 16th *arrondissement*. There were to be triple terraces rising to it from the Seine, and culminating in an immense colonnade with a frontage 400 metres long – freely imitating Mansart at Versailles. A project that dominated all salon conversation in Paris, it seems to have been, in the eyes of Lanzac de Laborie, the moment when Napoleon, giddy with military victory and on the brink of his ultimate folly – the march on Moscow – began 'to lose any sense of measure, to be haunted by unrealisable conceptions'. To Fontaine, he declared at the beginning of 1812: 'One must raise up new monuments, create a quarter filled with buildings whose grandeur and magnificence would wipe out everything that existed before.'

In terms of what it could have meant for Paris as a whole, this display of true *folie de grandeur* was distinctly alarming. In March 1812, Napoleon went on to decree the erection on the Left Bank by the Champ-de-Mars, opposite Chaillot, of three separate palaces for the archives and the university. As the Grande Armée was arriving in Smolensk, in 1812, the first stones were being laid. But by 1814, as the Allies were approaching Paris, only the foundations had been constructed – to be filled in by Louis XVIII in 1817. After the battle of Leipzig in 1813, Napoleon's gargantuan plans for Chaillot were reduced to one small square pavilion. Just as 'Aiglon', King of Rome, would never rule, so Chaillot would never be built. Yet, even during the Hundred Days, Fontaine and Percier were still receiving orders to take up the work again. And, in 1840, with 'the return of the ashes', Louis Philippe entertained thoughts of placing a tomb for Napoleon on the Trocadéro heights, instead of inside the Invalides.

Europe's most fearsome warlord since Genghis Khan, Napoleon left hecatombs of graves across Europe. Then, paradoxically, for all his ideas of the *embellissement* of Paris for the living, suddenly he found himself faced with the urgent problem of creating space for the grateful dead of Paris. By the end of the eighteenth century, the problem of burial inside the old city had become acute. Within its compressed confines, over-population of the dead presented a problem even more serious than that of housing the living. As space began to run out in the existing cemeteries, so the corpses of the poor were piled into common graves, usually several layers deep, from which an appalling smell pervaded the whole neighbourhood.

Napoleon's solution, in 1804, was to create a vast new cemetery out in the east end of Paris, on what had once been the leafy and agreeable estate belonging to the confessor of Louis XIV, Père Lachaise. His name now became immortalised as receptacle for all the great and the good of Paris's deceased. In its hundred acres lie notables ranging from Héloise and Abélard to Molière and Racine, from Napoleon's marshals to Chopin and de Musset, down to Sarah Bernhardt, Edith Piaf and Oscar Wilde in more modern times. Even today smart Parisians will all but kill to find a peaceful resting-place there. Altogether the tombs of Père Lachaise have come to represent the greatest agglomeration of architectural eccentricity in all Paris. Miniature pyramids rub shoulders with Gothic chapels, complete with gargoyles and lacy pinnacles. Hardly anything within living Paris has greater interest than the History-in-Marble that

Napoleon initiated up at Père Lachaise. In March 1814, Russian Cossacks were to fight their way into Paris through it; and in May 1871 it was where the Commune of Paris would hold its last bloody stand.

When the Corps Legislatif resumed session in the spring of 1806, its report on the state of the Empire (in fact dictated by Napoleon, and addressed to Napoleon) rang a note of extreme optimism: 'On your return to the capital your eyes will be struck by finding it more embellished in the course of a year of war than would have been achieved in half a century of peace.' The theme was repeated in the dark hours of 1813, when all the pillars were falling around him; but, in fact, throughout the duration of the Empire, Paris was described as resembling one vast building site. Including the Concorde, it was perpetually filled with piles of stone. When the King of Württemburg was asked, on a visit in 1810, what he thought of Paris, he replied tersely: 'Fine, for a town that the architects have taken by assault!'

At times Napoleon seemed close to despair over his plans for making his capital 'the most beautiful city in the world'. Essentially a man of the *midi*, there were several times when he contemplated escaping altogether from the negative attitude of the Parisians to found an entirely new capital in Lyons, 'a habitation worthy of my rank and fortune'. With due modesty, he thought of calling it 'Napoleonville'.

In carrying out his mammoth projects of *embellissement* in Paris, Napoleon attempted to run it all like a military department, and he also tried to maintain those principles of the *ancien régime* of 'rectitude, ordinance'. Unlike the *ancien régime*, however, he claimed never to lose sight of the financial problems. Louis XIV, he said, would never have been ruined had he known how to maintain a budget. His own was well regulated under the strict controls of the Ministry of the Interior;

Chaptal, the most important of his buildings' administrators, blamed the architects of the *ancien régime* for ruining Louis XIV. Nevertheless, in all Napoleon's vast building schemes, the estimates would always be set too low; his projects would be initiated on a staggering scale, which the faltering French economy could scarcely support at the same time as the requirements of endless war. Thus, by the time of Waterloo few would have been completed; his over-ambitious plans were terminated by defeat.

One of his most felicitous grand designs, the axis across the Concorde of the Madeleine and Palais Bourbon, with their echoing classical façades at each end, was not to find completion until a generation after Waterloo. Reverting to a church, the Madeleine failed to fulfil the Emperor's ambitions of creating a *Temple de la Gloire*, although it was to leave its eternal stamp on Paris. Arguably, Napoleon set an example of urban planning at its most enlightened and far-thinking. However, like many of Napoleon I's unfinished works, his overall scheme was to await its fruition under his nephew who, bolstered by the unstoppable and controversial Haussmann, was thus to prove himself perhaps superior as a city planner.

Typical were Napoleon's plans for Les Halles, which he condemned as 'unworthy of Paris!', or as a contemporary writer said of it in the year of Marengo:

'There is nothing more disgusting than the Halle à la Marée, the entrance to which is popularly known as the *porte merdeuse* ... The rotten planks of the stalls have been soaked for more than a century with the effluvia of decaying fish; fetid miasmas have seeped into the ground ... All in all it is a cesspool lying in one of the least airy districts of Paris.

He wanted a new complex to be ready by 1814; but, once again, he under-estimated the budget requirements – and time was running out. (In fact, it would take another century and a half and another authoritarian general to do something about Les Halles, when de Gaulle moved it all out to Rungis in 1969.)

Nevertheless, it could be justly claimed for Napoleon that he did transform Paris into an unrivalled centre of art and culture. It often seems that history has been unfair to him in leaving only one relatively narrow and short street named after him – Rue Bonaparte, in the VIème.

On the other hand, it may be also that Wellington should be thanked by Parisians for cutting Napoleon short before he could achieve some of his more dramatic ambitions: on St Helena, he declared that he would 'have got rid of any trace of "*ancien Paris*"; at Versailles he would have "chased away all those nymphs of such bad taste and replaced them with panoramas and masonry of all the capitals over which we had been victorious"'. He had cherished dreams of Paris becoming a city of two, three, four million inhabitants, 'something fabulous, colossal, unheard of in our day' and 'If only the Heavens had granted me another twenty years and some leisure, you would have looked in vain for the Old Paris; you would not have been able to see the slightest trace of it...' Perhaps the grateful Parisians should rename a significant Place after the Iron Duke, the city's saviour.

6   *Style by Decree*

My intention is to turn the arts especially towards subjects which
will tend to perpetuate the memory of what has been done in these
last fifteen years.

Napoleon to Daru, 1805

One aristocrat, Vicomtesse de Noailles, observed how much of
'old society', whose, property – and necks – had survived the
guillotine, dwelled in their horizontal apartments, apparently
in somewhat reduced circumstances: 'the dirty staircase,
common to all the inhabitants ... the few servants who still
worked were old and rather helpless; you always felt that they
had been such good company that their opinion was to be
respected'. Once inside the apartment, however, one felt oneself
'transported into another world, where, in the *petites chambres*,
everything was noble and well-cared for'.

In terms of the overall comfort of the bourgeoisie and former
aristocracy, however, things in Paris, at any rate, had changed
little since the days of Louis XIV. Plumbing was certainly no
better, nor was illumination. There was the new pump-lamp,
but that was reserved for special occasions; otherwise it was the
candle, which, costing four francs a pound, would be burnt –
literally – at both ends. One writer, Robiquet, described Imperial
Paris as 'not the City of Light, but the city of candle ends', while
the total number of street lights throughout Paris added up to
rather less than at the time of Louis XIV a century and a half
previously. Matches were not invented, and in circulation, till
1809. But the worst feature of life remained the winter cold. In
the Tuileries even Bonaparte was to be seen constantly wielding
a pair of fire-tongs; or, in the early morning, working with a

handkerchief tied around his head, its two corners flopping on to his shoulders.

What most distinguished the chic French interior as time went by under Napoleon was its furnishings. As Evangeline Bruce puts it, in the house of trend-setter Juliette Récamier on the fashionable *nouveau riche* Chaussée d'Antin, there could be found 'a riot of reproductions of the antique: of lions' muzzles and paws, of rams' feet and sphinxes, above all the Egyptian motifs'. Labelled *retour d'Egypt*, this latter had become the vogue since Napoleon's campaign there in 1798 – despite its failure and short duration. One minute the craze was all for polished wood; now it was all for things Egyptian. Not unnaturally, given the fundamental nature of the Empire, there was always a strong military influence; for instance, the bedroom of the actor Larive housed a camp bed set under a tent and surrounded with portraits of Spartacus and Genghis Khan, who featured among his most famous roles.

The *style Empire*, inseparable from the Napoleonic epic, signified a major departure in the history of French taste, breaking with the *douceur de vivre* of the *ancien régime*. In its constant reference to Egypt, Greece, Etruria and Rome, it sought to achieve a remarkable degree of homogeneity. It came to incorporate more of Imperial Rome than of Greece; while in fact its origins harked back to 1750, and the reign of Louis XV, with the exhumation of Pompeii. During the Egyptian campaign a visit to the Roman ruins at Pelusium had thrown up for Bonaparte a medallion of Julius Caesar, which he found 'a flattering omen'. There soon appeared a new medal showing Napoleon crowned with laurels.

Following the revolution, in the arts as in other fields, Bonaparte had been able to exploit the advantages of an empty slate. To his close associate Daru, in 1805, he admitted: 'My intention is to turn the arts especially towards subjects which will tend to perpetuate the memory of what has been done in these past

15 years.' And to Duroc, two years later: 'We must have very solid things, made to last a hundred years.' An official who offered him a Louis XVI cabinet was told brusquely that the Emperor 'wishes to create the new, not buy the old', while comments were scribbled on sketches of a candelabrum submitted by Percier: 'Simplify. This is for the Emperor.'

Napoleon's requirements of simplicity and solidity remain the salient characteristics of the Empire style. As a consequence particularly of the roots of Imperial Rome upon which it drew, there became, historically, a tendency to condemn *Empire* as being totalitarian and *nouveau riche*; nevertheless, being followed by a vacuum of taste under both Louis XVIII and Charles X, the style was to continue to be adopted, unashamedly, and long after the disappearance of the Emperor himself. On the collapse of 1815, it was even transported to New Jersey by Napoleon's brother Joseph, fleeing there as a refugee.

Some found the rectilinear severity of the *style Empire* more appropriate to the office of a general than to any intimacy. Certainly when one contemplates, in the famous painting by David, the uncomfortable pose of Mme Récamier on the *chaise longue* to which she gave her name, it becomes comprehensible how – on a piece of furniture offering so little prospect of a seduction *avec tous conforts* – she was able to preserve without difficulty that legendary virtue. In the words of Percier and Fontaine, the Empire's foremost stylists, the 'simple lines, pure contours, correct forms' borrowed from Pompeii and Herculaneum combined without too much problem with that of the Pharaonic, *retour d'Egypte* style. So too did the colours of the fiery poppy shade of red (derived, apparently, from the seeds of Egyptian field poppies that Bonaparte's men brought back in their boots from the Nile), and deep cockscomb red loved by the Bonapartes – because it was the colour of immortality. Thus heavy gilt sphinxes, griffins, lions' feet, bold eagles and Winged Victories symbolising military triumph predominated in the salons of Imperial France – and indeed, as already noted, preeminently at Josephine's Malmaison.

Then, under the influence of the women at the helm, once the rather macho store of republican Roman tales of virtue inherited from the revolutionary period had been exhausted, France turned with some relief to more romantic mythological themes, such as Cupid and Psyche. Often, bedroom ceilings would offer up Cupids floating ethereally to distract minds from the military motifs of the bed below. There was Pompeii, too, with swaying figures and silhouettes, 'discovered' from an age before the revolution. In 1814, regardless of the enemy approaching French territory, Napoleon presented a breakfast service to his stepson, Eugène de Beauharnais, depicting nymphs appearing before the tribunal of love.

In contrast to Josephine, Marie-Louise left no strong personal mark on the art of her time; objects associated with her are pleasing, comfortable and rich. News of the birth and baptism of the King of Rome, however, was to spur a vast new imagery in Paris and in the provinces; while the Emperor's bill from the mint, directed by Denon, for commemorative medals came to no less than 49,500 francs. They included a medallion showing the she-wolf nursing Romulus and Remus, founders of Rome. Influenced by Ancient Rome, Napoleon ordered the erasure of all red republican caps, symbols of liberty, that had been painted on public walls during the revolution ('I don't like to see such rubbish'). These were replaced by busts of Alexander and Frederick the Great, along with Brutus and Demosthenes.

Of all France's non-military enterprises, probably the decorative arts thrived most under Napoleon. The Lyons silk industry was revitalised to satisfy the copious demands of the Bonaparte family. Complementary colours such as yellow and purple would often be strikingly combined for floral borders of dresses, with a popular motif of palm fronds (again, the *retour d'Egypt* influence) and flowers. Imperial walls were lined with thousands of yards of Lyons silks. Napoleon urged his entourage to invest in French fabrics, notably silks manufactured in the brilliantly recreated factories at Lyons, of Camille Pernon, and the brothers Grand, or in the sumptuous damask embroideries of Joseph-Marie Jacquard. As a counter-measure against the British blockade, he decreed that costumes worn at court had to be made of French stuffs. There ladies were also supposed to renounce their imported cashmere shawls, though Josephine and Napoleon's sisters often defied this order.

The Empire was fortunate in being able to call upon an enormous existing class of artisans, well trained and hungry for employment after the lean days of the revolution. The metal workers of Paris and the Lyons silk weavers also formed large populations that were potentially troublesome when out of work. As the blockade threatened the artisans, so Napoleon responded by floating large loans to artists and entrepreneurs. In return they were required to guarantee to turn over a part of their output worth more than the amounts they had been advanced. Thus, by 1807 Jacob-Desmalter, Napoleon's favourite furniture-maker, operating under the influence of designs by his top architects, Percier and Fontaine, was employing no fewer than 350 craftsmen; while his fellow artisan, Thomire, had up to 800 men working at moments of peak activity. Denon even had designed for the Emperor's medals a cabinet in the shape of an Egyptian stylus, encrusted with Napoleonic bees. Until supplies ran out, there was a strong taste for massive mahogany imported from Cuba. The 'boat' or 'gondola' bed, the fancy imported from conquered Venice, made its appearance. For a long time heavy ormolu from the days of Louis XIV remained in fashion by way of embellishment. There were candelabra grotesquely ornamented with winged victories, rams' heads, blindfolded girls and serpents that held up the shade in their mouths, by Ravrio – who set up a prize for anyone who could discover a way of protecting workers from the poisonous vapours produced by gilding with mercury (an interesting concern about welfare of the work-force even then.)

In gold and silver work, among 900 silversmiths working in Paris during the Empire, Napoleon had Auguste working hard for him, who in 1804 constructed a special tureen which, as an indication of the continuity of patronage and style between monarchy and Empire, repeated a model he had first produced back in 1790. From Auguste, Napoleon commissioned a tiara as a gift to Pius VII on the occasion of the coronation. Then there was Martin-Guillaume Biennais, formerly a cabinet-maker who later became official silversmith to the imperial couple. Over the years Napoleon ordered as presents – often for his female conquests – dozens of gold boxes; no fewer than one hundred from Marguerite's workshop alone. Under the Empire, Auguste and his colleagues gradually began to turn from the worked to the plain surface, shifting their art from chasing and engraving to cast figural handles, plaques and pedestals in a kind of sculpted abstraction. Everywhere Empire furniture showed an obsession with gilt clawed feet, suggesting the influence of militaristic triumphalism.

Swiftly after the Consulate became Empire, there was a notable change in the style of dress, away from the Greco-Roman imitations of the Directoire – those high-waisted, low-cut dresses that so impressed English gentlemen; and as gauzily transparent as minimal decency would allow. Young women were now warned not to stand against the light 'the beautiful orb that illumes us'; while, in contrast to days of the Directoire, the excessively undressed might be booed in public. It was Josephine who led the way. As in all things, the orders came down from the top. For a while the daring nudity of the Directoire prevailed; then Napoleon, the Mediterranean, let it be known that he wished to suppress 'this masquerade of gallantry'. He required

Napoleon Bonaparte, 1769–1821, as 1st Consul. A copy of a lost 1803 portrait.

Left A Parisian salon in the Directoire era, 1795–99. An engraving after Jean-Francois Bosio.

Josephine de Beauharnais at Malmaison in 1800, painted by Francois Gérard.

Jean-Jacques-Régis de Cambacérès, 1753–1824, Chancellor of the Empire.

Left Château de Malmaison, painted by Pierre Joseph Petit.

Napoleon and Marie-Louise enter the Tuileries Gardens on the day of their wedding, 2nd April 1810, painted by Étienne-Barthélemy Garnier.

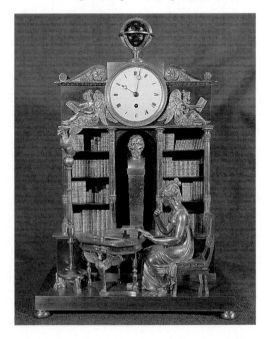

Napoleonic lady in her *bibliothèque* (note the Empire furnishings). Mantel clock by Ravrio, *c.* 1810.

Walking with the baby King of Rome, heir of Napoleon and Marie-Louise, on the Tuileries terrace. An engraving by Dubois.

'The Man With Six Heads', a caricature of Charles Maurice de Talleyrand-Perigord, 1754–1838.

Madame de Staël, 1766–1817, leading woman of letters in opposition to Napoleon.

The new Rue de Rivoli in Paris.

Johann Wolfgang von Goethe,
1749–1832, German poet and
playwright, in the Roman
countryside, painted by Johan
Tischbein.

A view of the stage at the Paris Opéra, located in the Rue Richelieu
1794–1820.

Napoleon's tomb on the island of Saint Helena.

women in general, not only of the court, to be less naked. Josephine's fun-loving friend, Thérèse Tallien, was ticked off for appearing as a particularly seductive, semi-clad Diana at the opera. Josephine was required to provide the example with a 'relative severity in her attire'.

In 1804, at a presentation of the Légion d'Honneur, Josephine had appeared clad dazzlingly in rose-coloured tulle, sewn with silver stars, her hair 'crowned with dozens of diamond wheat ears'. Some considered it a bit over the top; then, the following year, after Austerlitz, as Josephine continued to wear the deepest *décolletés*, if Napoleon deemed it indecent he would tear it off her and throw it into the fire. She never protested, but 'calmly sent for another one, since she owned hundreds,' says Evangeline Bruce. On another occasion, just to make sure he would not see a certain pink and silver lamé number again, Napoleon threw a bottle of ink over it – even though Josephine was already dressed for a reception. She put up with a lot.

To Napoleon dress was always partly a symbol of power and glory. But it also had economic and commercial implications. As the British blockade of the continent bit deeper, Napoleon decreed that the border of a lady's train could not exceed four inches, and it had to be made from French cloth: Napoleon did his best to augment the trade of native silk manufacturers and designers.

Aided by Josephine's couturier, Leroy, who operated from one corner of the Rue Ménars (now a modest street in the 2nd *arrondissement*'s business section), dresses under the Empire also became heavier: 'sleeves short and puffed, the tunic falling straight, moulding the forms without stressing them'. Thus, in this so-called 'sincerity fashion', the historian Robiquet observes that 'an ugly woman becomes more so, a pretty woman looks prettier, a really beautiful woman scores a triumph'. It was also said, unkindly, that as Josephine's figure expanded with the years, the fashions contrived to 'make her look stouter still'. In an age of no crinoline or bustles, trickery was impossible.

Naturally, the heavier dresses also became more expensive. A quite ordinary dress for the Empress would cost ff3000; her bill (*chez* Leroy) for one year would amount to ff143,314, 10 centimes (note the 10 centimes!); and when her wardrobe was inventoried in 1809, it totalled 666 winter dresses, 230 summer ones – and, *toujours la Créole!* – only two pairs of knickers. An enormous amount of money was spent on rouge (ff3000 a year for Josephine), as Napoleon hated pale women. Then there was the 'medieval' mode known as the *style troubadour*, which greatly influenced late Empire fashion – as displayed by Ingres's portrait of Mme Alexandre Léthière, with her daughter, Letizia, wearing a plaid dress with ruff and long sleeves. Despite the chauvinism bred by war, there was also much emulation by the smart Parisienne of hats *à l'Anglaise* – huge 'poke' bonnets. Fur shops did a roaring trade with lynx and ermine brought in from eastern Europe; but the rarest, and therefore most sought-after, were chinchillas originating from South America, cut off by British blockade – there were said to be only twenty skins left in the whole of Europe.

As for the men, dress had also sobered down considerably from the modes of the *incroyables* handed down from the Directoire. In February 1805, a young Stendhal describes himself as never having been 'so brilliant': 'I was wearing a black waistcoat, black silk breeches and stockings, with a cinnamon-bronze coat, a very well tied cravat, a superb shirt-front. Never, I believe, was my ugliness more effaced by my general appearance ... I looked a very handsome man, after the style of Talma.' Wearing such an attire, he could probably just as well have paraded passably down St James's without being taken for a French spy. On the other hand, there was the camp Cambacérès, his suit of cloth of gold 'lighting up the whole salon'. Sometimes the Napoleonic generals, especially those of plebeian origins – like Lefebvre – looked distinctly out of place in their fancy rigs.

*

To a sensible extent, under the Empire dress reflected morals – and vice versa. Napoleon wanted his subjects to dress more modestly, and be more moral. An advertisement in a paper of 1804, by a woman wishing 'to enter into legal union with a man of good morals', suggests that to some extent the Emperor may have been successful; though one may well question just how far his interest resided in a desire to raise the nation's birthrate – to provide more soldiers. As it was, war created a new and immensely profitable industry – the marriage bureau. Here an unscrupulous Monsieur Vuillaume made a fortune, keeping a check on names of men killed in battle; unfortunately his grisly work led him ultimately to the lunatic asylum at Charenton: 'yet another victim of marriage?' commented the wits. Meanwhile, in the countryside, Mme de Chateaubriand could observe that 'Nobody in Chatenay expected a girl to be a girl on her wedding day.'

For Napoleon himself, and his family – naturally – a different code applied, as has already been seen. His sisters, Pauline Borghese and Caroline Murat, lived fast and loose; so too did many of the marshals and their wives – not least Laure Junot, Duchesse d'Abrantès, who, having once rejected the Emperor himself at Malmaison, then took the bit between her teeth. Leading from the front, the Emperor himself could take a mistress, or cast off a wife, just as the spirit moved him. Summing up on the customs of the age, one English expert on style, James Laver, observes that 'certainly the morals of the Napoleonic epoch were no better than those of the *ancien régime*, and its manners not nearly so good'.

The English press, conceivably influenced by the prejudices of war, assessed the number of prostitutes in the Paris of 1806 as high as 75,000. With not enough room in the prisons for them, the police were alleged to be powerless to act 'against such an army'. That same year of 1806, a new law proscribed gambling – but with a convenient escape clause: 'except for places where mineral waters are found ... and for the city of

Paris'. As it had done since the most *louche* days of the Regent, Philippe Duc d'Orléans, in the early eighteenth century, the centre of raffish life, pleasure and vice in Paris continued to centre around Richelieu's Palais-Royal. One of the cross-Channel visitors hastening to it during the Peace of Amiens depicted it as 'a horrible scene of debauch situated in the midst of a great city, which has corrupted and rotted the whole society'. Con-men (one of their easy victims, in 1807, was the court painter David), pickpockets and shameless tarts proliferated there – the lower-class ones dragging off their clients behind the poulterers' sheds in the nearby market-place. Equally rapacious were the gambling dens on the Palais-Royal, where (in the words of Balzac in *La Peau de Chagrin*) it was said that customers could, in the space of a few hours, be ruined, commit suicide (courtesy of the gunsmith next door) and pass to a better world with the aid of one of the defrocked priests attendant at the non-stop party. Smutty bookshops abounded, and there was little difficulty locating a group orgy. From time to time these would be raided by Fouché's police; but, as in the era of the Marquis de Sade, the men would be allowed to go free, only the women arrested.

As is so frequently the story with autocratic regimes, with the passage of time, corruption set in. At the top, starting from a zero base, all the Bonaparte family amassed considerable fortunes – either from loot obtained abroad or by other means. Napoleon's sister, Pauline Borghese, was able to acquire one of the most sumptuous houses in Paris, on the Faubourg Saint-Honoré. To the lasting benefit of Britain, the Duke of Wellington bought it after Waterloo. He gained the respect of Parisians, when, as the victor, he could have grabbed it for nothing, but insisted on paying the full market price. It remains the British Embassy, grandest of them all.

Josephine, the penniless Creole, in 1809, the year before Napoleon divorced her, could count hundreds of different dresses;

Cambacérès, Napoleon's Chancellor, could afford to strut around the Palais-Royal dressed like a millionaire peacock, an early day Field-Marshal Goering; Talleyrand, also a self-made man, as we have already seen, had no hesitation about playing the markets with inside knowledge to amass vast wealth. Lower down the scale, Louis Dubois, the much despised city Prefect, was reputed to slip VD 'dispensary tax' – in fact, protection money received from prostitutes – into his desk drawer.

The pompous Prefect might claim in his inaugural manifesto 'My eye shall penetrate the innermost recesses of the criminal soul', yet – despite the efforts of the ubiquitous Fouché, supported by all the trappings of a police state – lawlessness continued to persist in Napoleonic Paris. With army deserters and even senior officers involved, and as shortages grew, so smuggling became a major industry, run like a military operation. Tunnels a quarter of a mile long were dug under the city customs *barrières*, discovered emerging beneath a convent. By 1808 the situation had become so bad that, as with the Berlin Wall of the 1960s, a ban was imposed on any building or construction work within a hundred yards of the city perimeter. But still it went on.

One of the plagues of Paris under the Consulate had been the multitude of beggars. One German visitor was profoundly

> moved by the horrible, endless begging in the streets ... in bad, dirty weather, when one cannot step too far away from the houses without ending up in a sea of sludge, or when one is in danger of falling under a wheel, one has to make one's way through long rows of beggars who cannot be avoided...

There were reported to be over 100,000 in 1802, and the figure did not decrease by the end of the Empire. Many were discharged old soldiers, reproaching civilians with their silent salutes. In 1809, the Paris police declared its intention of creating a huge home for beggars outside the city at Villers-Cotterets. But nothing was ever done. Meanwhile much of the incidental robbery and violence on the streets of Paris was caused by licentious soldiery on leave, deserters, or draft-dodgers. There were numerous ways of avoiding the call to arms, such as chopping off a finger or knocking out front teeth, without which a soldier could not tear open a musket cartridge. It was reckoned that no fewer than one in ten recruits managed to escape the Napoleonic recruiting sergeant, while in 1806, the year of Jena, only 14,300 Parisians were serving out of a population of nearly 600,000 – extraordinary, when one considers how the very survival of the Empire depended on the manpower of its Grande Armée.

By 1810 the rate of desertions had become alarming, with many deserters taking refuge among the criminal underclass in Paris. Parisians might applaud the handsome veterans when they paraded on the Carrousel – but for the rest of the time they were the terror of Paris, recognised for their brutality against inoffensive citizens. A soldier relieved himself on to guests in an underground café, and, when a waiter reproached him, he was beaten up. Six soldiers raped a respectable woman at the Port-au-Blé, then threw her into the Seine. When a staff officer made a pass at a shopkeeper's daughter and the father remonstrated 'Monsieur, my daughter is an honest girl!', 'So much the better – that's how I like them' was the arrogant response. In the shadows, Fouché's minions also fought a ruthless war against spies, or suspected spies, financed by English gold. One was a famed Royal Navy captain, John Wesley Wright, a special agent who disappeared into the dread Temple prison in May 1805, to be discovered in his cell on 28 October with his throat cut, in his hand a *closed* razor. His friends in the Navy suspected he might have been murdered in reprisal for Trafalgar.

Continuing grinding poverty often had much to do with Napoleon's lust for conquest, and his concomitant requirement for more and more soldiers, mounting as the battles proliferated. Typical was this plea of hardship passed to the Emperor from the 71-year-old widow of an officer, and mother of the commanding officer of a battalion in Spain; the son was keeping her in her old age but was absent abroad for long periods, whence she received no news: 'Deprived of every kind of help, and weighed down by age and infirmity,' ran the official report to Napoleon, 'she has hope only in the generosity of Your Excellency.'

In general, Napoleon endeavoured to be receptive to the plight of the poor, soldiers and their dependants in particular; it was part of his mystique, and in his own interest. Under the revolution, typically of the workings of revolutionary socialism in practice, the soup kitchens had been cruelly suppressed – especially during years of famine. Then, from 1800 onwards, Napoleon had recreated the *soupes économiques* (a notion borrowed from the English). Among his own personal charities for the poor, on the announcement of the pregnancy of Marie-Louise in November 1810, he decreed the allocation of ff250,000 to help their indebtedness. Nevertheless, swollen by the deserters, the underclass of most French cities, but notably the Paris poor, lived as miserably as ever they had under the *ancien régime*. In the early days, prices of foodstuffs had been kept artificially, and ridiculously, low. So had drink prices. Then, as the British blockade tightened its grip, so prices soared; notably in that essential luxury, sugar.

In Paris there were areas of pronounced sordid misery around the Hôtel Dieu, in the Faubourg Saint-Marceau, and in the 12th *arrondissement* where, in 1813, one-fifth of the population were listed as indigent. Conditions in these poorer *quartiers* were appalling; one contemporary observer, Mouret de Chaume, wrote:

> The extreme overcrowding of residents in certain quarters, and the stench of the household animals blended with that of

excrement, decaying animal cadavers, and rotting food, all create extensive atmospheric pollution in which people live and eat. The fetid air is a visible haze that generally covers Paris and there are districts over which it is particularly thick.

As it always had, in Napoleonic France poverty marched hand in hand with disease. On a visit to the Hotel Dieu in November 1801, Chaptal had been profoundly shocked by the lack of hygiene, the disorder and the hideous dirt and dilapidation he had found. He succeeded in persuading the Paris Council to relocate pregnant women and sick children, and above all the mentally ill, elsewhere. Hitherto sick children of the working classes had been mixed in with adults in ordinary hospitals – greatly to their detriment. Relaxation of morals under the revolution had resulted in a galloping increase in venereal disease, euphemistically known as *les maladies honteuses*, which had demanded the creation of a special hospital in the vacant Capucin monastery in the Faubourg Saint-Jacques. At first called simply the Hospital of the Vénériens, then – later, in the delicate nineteenth century – the Hôpital du Midi, the Vénériens had an enormous waiting-list, two months long, to get treatment.

Nevertheless, by the end of the Empire, considerable strides had been made to improve the medieval conditions in Paris hospitals. On Napoleon's accession, there had been the three main establishments – the Hôtel Dieu, La Verité and Saint-Louis; by the time of his fall, the capital counted no less than eleven hospitals with an average of 5,392 beds occupied, the number of beds having increased by over a thousand. There were acceptably modest charges of 120–130 centimes a day, First Class (allocated by the Emperor as a reward for services); Second Class, for the over 70s – 80 centimes; Third Class – 50 centimes. Here, as with so much else in Imperial Paris, places were allocated by the Prefect of Police. Orphanages (orphans were '*enfants trouvés*') had been created and a special hospital for '*enfants malades*' opened in the Rue de Sèvres. Similar facilities existed in provincial cities.

All through his time in power, Napoleon remained constantly haunted by fears of troubles from the *classes laborieuses* in the cities, of another '89. What in fact kept them quiet, through years of great privation? One reason was the ubiquitousness and efficiency of Fouché's (and later Savary's) secret police. Secondly, there was the mystical allure of the Grande Armée (especially while it won battles), which provided both jobs and *gloire*, and the heady prospects of the baton in the knapsack in this notionally classless society, of rewards like the 'baubles' of the Légion d'Honneur. Thirdly, there was the skilful application of 'bread and circuses', continuing even after the end of the military victories, with the seemingly indestructible mystique of Emperor and Empire. On top of this, in general terms, was the remarkable fact of how little life in France, and particularly Paris, was affected by the long-drawn-out war. There were the great *défilés* after victories like Marengo; there was scarcity of various categories of food and raw materials; otherwise, however, life went on little affected by the war. There were the distractions of the new galleries in the Louvre, the new building works, the promenades, the theatre, the opera – and no serious press to report unpleasant realities from far-flung battlefields.

One is reminded somewhat of Irving Shaw's masterpiece of the 1950s, *The Young Lions*, recounting how everyday life in Hitler's Berlin was relatively insouciant of the war in the early years after 1939 – until the bombing began in earnest. And Napoleon's Paris was never bombed. Even the loss of the Grande Armée in the retreat from Moscow in 1812 hardly disturbed the rhythm of life. Only the actual appearance of Cossacks on the Champs-Élysées in 1814 could do that.

All of these factors contrived to obscure from the French

proletariat the one inescapable, and singularly unpalatable, truth – that they had *lost* the Great Revolution that had been launched by them, and for them.

7 The Pleasures of Empire

> There is nothing which compares to Corneille, or to Racine. There
> is no way of reading one of his [Shakespeare's] plays, they make one
> sorry for him...
>
> **Napoleon commenting on the theatre, 1803**

Coexisting closely side by side with so much poverty and
misery, and despite the high reformist ambitions of the Empire,
the old aristocracy – those who had not lost their heads –
and the *haute bourgeoisie* had recouped their fortunes most
miraculously. Meanwhile, a new class of *nouveaux riches*,
which included the imperial family and its hangers-on, had
arisen from the ashes of the revolution with astonishing speed.
As it had after many other upheavals in French history, before
and after, the bourgeoisie had shown particular resilience. Under
the Empire its ascendancy was epitomised by the Récamiers,
bloodied but unbowed from the 1805 bank crash, from which
they had recovered with amazing swiftness – as indeed the
bourgeoisie always seemed to.

The Récamiers lived in the Chaussée d'Antin, fringeing on
some of the more underprivileged parts of Paris. It was the house
where once had lived Louis XVI's ill-starred Minister of Finance,
Swiss-born Jacques Necker, who was in office when the revolution broke out and who was also father of Germaine de Staël,
one of Napoleon's most persistent critics. From her legendary
salon there, Juliette Récamier dispensed lavish hospitality.
Daughter of a Lyons solicitor, financed by an elderly banker
husband (whom she married at sixteen), and closest (perhaps
only) friend of Mme de Staël, she presided over a worldly shrine,
its décor setting the standards of *Empire* style. Juliette with her

great and serene beauty – which seemed to embody the period's ideal of feminine perfection – inspired many passions, unfulfilled until Chateaubriand came along and picked the lock. 'Mme Récamier has,' wrote J. F. Reichardt, an impressionable German, 'such a throughly translucent skin that one can see the blood course through her veins ... her beautiful mouth, full of fine teeth, is always half-open; she seems to find it quite natural that people like to look at her in the same position and pose for hours on end' – notably on the excruciatingly uncomfortable sofa to which she lent her name.

In a society that was 'frivolous and passibly corrupted' ('frivole et passablement corrompue'), as Laborie described it, she seemed sometimes like an unassailable amulet of virtue in a sea of adultery – 'never happy, never in despair'. As a token of her moral unassailability (even Lucien Bonaparte had been led on, and rejected) she would greet each newly arrived lady with the invitation: 'Voulez-vous voir ma chambre à coucher?' Walls covered with mirrors, there was a statue to *Silence*, lit by a lamp into which a genie poured drops of oil. Cocottes would copy the famous bed, adorning it with crossed lances and a shield by way of a memento of liaisons with Grande Armée heroes, but Juliette's *chambre* was nevertheless, according to the uncharitable gossips, a bedroom where nothing happened – and where, said the *mauvaises langues*, she preserved her virginity even from Monsieur Récamier (it was rumoured that he was in fact her true father). So popular was her salon that Napoleon once quipped about moving the seat of government there.

As well as setting the tone in *salon* life, dress and furnishings, Mme Récamier also played an important part in reviving the culinary arts in Paris. With the end of the Terror, there had been a proliferation of restaurants in Paris, opened by chefs of the *grands seigneurs* who had lost their jobs – just as their bosses lost their heads. Already by 1798, there were an estimated 2000 restaurateurs in the city. Many, like Véry on the site of the former Feuillant Convent, off the new Rue de Rivoli, or the Grand Véfour behind the Palais-Royal (today living considerably off its past fame), depended on the patronage of Empress Josephine. At the former, the 'splendid Mme Véry sat enthroned like Juno on her *estrade* [platform]'. There was Chez Noudet, also in the Palais-Royal and not far from the Récamiers, which in 1813 cheered up Paris with the secrets of *brandades de morue* – the greatest gastronomic success of the time. At the top end of the scale, one could also dine at the grand Hôtel de Courland, close to where the present – and equally grand – Crillon stands; though Reichardt complained that there one was 'skinned alive'. In the eyes of Balzac they were also hotbeds of lust and debauchery.

At the lower end of the scale, there were the plentiful plebeian *bastringues* and *guinguettes*, outside the *barrières* where one danced on a grass lawn. Then there were the cafés, the most frequented being in the Palais-Royal, but also the much sought-after Café de Paris, on the Pont-Neuf where the old statue of Henri IV once stood; popular, too, was the unusual Café des Aveugles with its orchestra composed entirely of the blind. Between 6 and 9 p.m., Parisian bachelors would spend several hours in such cafés; often they would be noisy places with soldiers on leave killing time (sometimes each other), shouting from one end of the room to the other.

Under the Empire, eating times and habits changed. Before the revolution there was a proverb that '*déjeuner* was for friends, *dîner* was for etiquette; afternoon tea [*goûter*] for children, and the *souper* for love'. Now, the old routine of *dîner* at 4 p.m. was abandoned by the chic for the more modern time of 7 p.m. The *dîner* would usually finish at 9, exceptions to the rule among the élite being Cambacérès whose yawn-making dinners would often drag on for five hours, and Napoleon himself who, from military habit, found 15–20 minutes long enough for any meal.

There was no regular dining room in the Tuileries, so he would give orders each morning where the table was to be laid, and in which room. Little interested in food (he devoured everything at hand, swiftly and indiscriminately – fish, flesh or sweet dishes), the Emperor fancied good wine; his favourites were Chambertin, Clos-Vougeot and Château-Lafite.

Those who, like Mme Récamier, were keen on the *bonne table* would consult Grimod de la Reynière and his famed *Almanach des Gourmands*, a forerunner of the *Guide Michelin* which bracketed the fat years of the Empire (1803–12). In the *Almanach* you could learn how to prepare a *gigot*; it had to be 'looked forward to like a lovers' first rendez-vous, beaten as tender as a liar caught in the act, blonde as a German girl and bleeding like a Carib. Mutton is to lamb what the millionaire uncle is to a poverty-stricken nephew ... spinach is the virgin wax of cookery ...'

By 1812, however, when the *Almanach* closed down, all Paris was tightening its belts as, with the blockade by *perfide Albion* becoming ever more effective, gourmets found essential ingredients rarer and rarer. Almost no rum, coffee, chocolate or sugar was coming in from the French West Indies. Even imperial dignitaries were known to suspend a piece of sugar on a string from the ceiling, each member of the family allowed to dip it in their cup only briefly.

Despite austerity imposed by the war outside, imperial society was renowned for its parties, receptions and balls. Napoleon, characteristically, did everything on the grandest scale, planned as always like a major military operation. There were five, and only five, imperial receptions mounted at the Hôtel de Ville attended by Napoleon, each a nightmare for the party planners. The first, two weeks after the coronation, on 16 December 1804, caused a major traffic jam, with 6000 coaches all snarled up. Even princes and marshals had to wait four to five hours before they could get away – a situation that would be unusual even in twenty-first-century Paris!

A huge ball was thrown in August 1808, to mark the Emperor's birthday – but conviviality was somewhat dampened by news of a first Napoleonic humiliation, and General Dupont's capitulation at Bailen in Spain. *En revanche*, the following autumn – on his way back from Wagram, which, though his last triumph, appeared as sensational as ever – Napoleon instructed the unfortunate Prefect Frochot to prepare a reception for 3000 guests, the moment he returned to Paris. Overwhelmed, Frochot replied that a party on that scale would take a month to organise. Fortunately for him, and his continuity in office, Napoleon changed his mind and eventually the dinner was fixed for the first Sunday in December, to mark Austerlitz Day. On the appointed evening, the numbers in fact exceeded 4000; Napoleon sat down with five kings on his right, Josephine and her mother, and four queens or princesses on his left. There followed a ball, with a quadrille opened by crowned heads of state. It cost ff3 million, but as Napoleon explained, he wanted 'to come and dine in the house of my good city, and thus to give her a stunning testimony of my love'. Certainly few other French rulers could afford to rival such a display of regal affection. Two years later, celebrating the birth of the King of Rome at the Hôtel de Ville – a more muted affair, given the downward turn in the fortunes of the Empire – Napoleon, apparently in imitation of an old German custom, dined solemnly with his crown balanced on his head.

Evidently *fêtes* at the Tuileries were even more portentous, starchier affairs. At a ball given on 20 April 1806, for the marriage of Stephanie de Beauharnais, 2500 guests were divided into two groups and therefore two concurrent balls. Each was convinced that theirs was for the bourgeois, and that the truly smart party was elsewhere. At a ball in February 1812 the discontent of Parisian society was multiplied by strict demarcation between the personnel of the court, who were the only ones allowed to join in the dancing, and the bourgeois, who could only look on. They were not even allowed to fill up their plates at the buffet; instead food was brought to them in their isolated *loges*.

There was a terrible stiffness about all balls given by the Emperor, possibly rivalled only by those of the ridiculous, gay peacock, Chancellor Cambacérès. Of one such, in 1807, a lonely lady of the court wrote: 'There were plenty of women here, but very few dancers and without utilising the pages whom we brought I really don't know what would have happened...!' Cambacérès, however, seemed in no way distressed if his lady guests remained 'mute and immobile', or offended if they departed on the dot of 8.30 – heading for a party of Napoleon's favourite sister, Pauline Borghese, or Talleyrand.

These were the most sought-after hosts of the Empire; at Neuilly in June 1810, celebrating his wedding to Marie-Louise, Pauline put her brother totally in the shade with what was described as a 'fête de nuit féerique'. Wicked old Talleyrand, the defrocked bishop who employed the noted chef Carême, always gave parties that were fun; partly because of the gambling that went on, but notably because of the gorgeous women, of whom the famous diarist Mme Rémusat said that they were 'more often lovers than friends'. At such gatherings, people forgot how drab the rare dances had been during the revolution, or how orgiastic they had become during the Directoire. Instead, first there was the waltz imported from Vienna, then the mazurka introduced from Poland, in 1807 (together with Marie Walewska). Enormously popular was Julien's dance orchestra – sometimes made to work so hard that he was once found to be fast asleep over his violin at five in the morning. In contrast were the parties given by Talleyrand's rival, the sinister Fouché, where one British diplomat noted the 'bad style of the company ... muddy boots, doubtful linen'.

*

Under the Empire, walking became a new-found pleasure, 'even for fair ladies not accustomed to showing themselves', declared the *Journal de Paris* in 1808. A new chic promenade opened up near the Récamiers on the Chaussée d'Antin; strollers could then refresh themselves with ices at Frascati or the Jardin Turc, a large café with shady terraces, where they would be entertained by tight-rope walkers and tumblers – much as outside the Centre Pompidou today. Then, for the less pretentious Parisian there were frequent circuses, dancing by moonlight, fireworks, balloon ascents and every form of innocent entertainment out at the Tivoli Gardens, close to today's Gare Saint-Lazare. All good innocent fun, studiously devoid of any political content.

But still, perhaps even more than in the days of Louis XIV, it was the theatre that attracted all classes of Parisian as an essential element of their daily pleasure. Julien-Louis Geoffroy (1743–1814), the leading drama critic of the era, reckoned that – after the dead years of the revolution – under the Consulate the taste for the theatre had virtually grown into a *fureur*. Damned by Laborie as a 'morose moralist', servile to the government, and capable of brutal cruelty to young actresses, Geoffroy feared that – rather like modern television – taken to excess, the contemporary vogue for the stage could lead to 'a total distaste for conversation and domestic pleasures, and a kind of annihilation of the spirit'.

Ever since the days of the great Corneille two centuries earlier, and certainly under Louis XIV's Molière and Racine, France had been addicted to the theatre, more ever than England. With the aristocracy and the bourgeoisie cowering in their cellars from the attentions of Madame Guillotine, it was perhaps surprising that, during the revolution, the Paris theatre could find any audience. Regarded by the Convention as a breeding place for *incivisme*, it had become a fairly muted affair. But with the Directoire it had sprung into life again. As for Napoleon, there was barely any other aspect of life there in which he interfered more – and often not very helpfully. For instance, from Milan in 1805, Napoleon told Fouché to scrub a new play about Henri IV, because he thought 'this period is still not far enough away so as not to arouse passions ... I think that you should prevent it, without showing your intervention.' In particular, he objected to the words, in the heroic king's mouth, 'je tremble ...'; for a sovereign, he declared, 'may be afraid, but must never say so'.

In the middle of the Polish campaign, while preparing to enter Warsaw in the winter of 1806, Napoleon somehow found time to criticise the interpretation of a new play, telling Fouché that the distinguished author Raynouard – who was Perpetual Secretary of the Academie, no less – had got it wrong in *Les Templiers*, missing the point of *raison d'état*. (Young Stendhal's appraisal of *Les Templiers*: 'mortally boring'.) It would have been better, opined Napoleon, if – in burning the Templars – the cruel medieval king Philippe le Bel should be shown as having 'played a noble role ... then one would understand that he could not have acted differently'. Instead of being depicted as a 'tyrant', he should appear as 'the saviour of nation'. It was a critique that possibly told one less about the play than about Napoleon's own morality – as it did on another occasion when Napoleon was heard to pass judgement on Oedipus; one should not be too hasty, he declared, before considering as to whether 'necessity might provide justification'.

While encamped in Tilsit in faraway East Prussia, he insti-gated a decree forbidding actors of the Imperial Theatre to act on any other stage; the word 'prison' was even pronounced. All too frequently Napoleon would ban plays he did not like, ask for lines to be altered, or – at twelve hours' notice – request the great Talma to perform *Britannicus* instead of *Phèdre*, without bothering to enquire whether or not the troupe knew their parts. Repeatedly the top theatre companies would be ordered, at short notice, to put on command performances for the imperial entourage – at Compiègne, at Fontainebleau and as far afield as Germany. When Talma and the top stars were dispatched to entertain the international conference at Erfurt in 1808, there were complaints from Paris at their prolonged absence, to which Napoleon replied, 'Oh well, let them leave their understudies behind!' On the same occasion, Napoleon told Goethe, on a first meeting with his great fan, somewhat condescendingly: 'During your stay here, you must spend every evening at our *spectacles*. It won't do you any harm to see performed good French tragedies ... In my box you'll meet a good number of sovereigns ... and you'll see the archbishop sleeping on the shoulder of the King of Württemberg...!'

Five years later, in 1813, in the middle of the critical Battle of Nations that he was to lose, Napoleon would request Cambacérès to send the Comédie-Française all the way to Dresden – not only to '*faire du bruit à Paris*, but also to have a good effect in London and Spain, and make people believe that we are amusing ourselves in Dresden. There is little enough comedy in the situation here...' Seventeen actors were duly dispatched, at enormous cost, arriving just as the Grande Armée faced one of its most decisive defeats. Though it could be argued that it was better to have a sovereign showing an interest in the theatre than the reverse, undoubtedly Napoleon's constant interference (and, on occasion, Josephine interfered too) caused great damage.

Progressively as Napoleon consolidated his power, he showed himself less and less tolerant of the media. The hand of the censor became heavier. On his return from Tilsit in 1807, he told Fouché that one newspaper – the official *Moniteur* – was quite sufficient, there was no need for others. When he came to power, Paris alone could boast over seventy newspapers; within a year these had been reduced to thirteen, all under strict censorship. The once lively press became uninformative and as dull as dishwater. Following Trafalgar, Stendhal's diaries typically reveal how little he was able to glean about political developments in Europe, or about commercial pressures in Europe, from his reading of Paris journals – and how little impact it had upon him. Swiftly censorship spread to books and plays as well, where any allusion to politics was forbidden. Fouché's spies were everywhere; all at court were required to report on each other, with suspects promptly arrested.

At the same time that Napoleon ordered the reduction of papers, he instructed that the overall number of theatres be reduced to eight. As a result, between fifteen and twenty *petits théâtres* in Paris were closed down. In addition to pleading financial expediency, this was also an effective means of controlling any likelihood of subversive propaganda on the stage. With the curtain usually rising at 6 p.m., all performances were required to end around 9.30, by police order, so as to make the journey home through darkened streets less menacing. In everything, the police presence – under despised Prefect Dubois – made itself felt. By decree of 1806, no new play could be performed without the authority of the minister. There were severe penalties for actors failing to clock in for a performance because of sudden laryngitis; they could be imprisoned or confined in an abbey or convent. The *Surintendant de Spectacles*, Rémusat (husband of the well-known diarist), could award a sentence of up to a week. Beyond that it had to be confirmed by the Emperor himself, or defaulting players could be embarrassed by appearing in police reports, such as: 'Madame Chevigny was at her country house with a young man aged 24, a little-known individual ...'

High-handed as such treatment may sound, the theatre managers had plenty of good excuses; Parisian *vedettes* of the time, the Talmas, were notoriously resistant to discipline and would think little of taking a night off. Even the Talmas were not immune, while Napoleon's favourite, the irresistible Mlle

George, found herself in the summer of 1808 fined ff3000 for non-appearance, expelled from a number of societies and forfeiting her pension rights. In a world where the theatre was only just recovering from the undignified agit-prop absurdities that it witnessed during the more *enragé* moments of the revolution, there was also no shortage of semi-literate bureaucrats to carry out the work of censorship, which often ascended to the heights of the ridiculous.

The new stage morality was defined by toady critic Geoffroy: 'People are determined to have virtue on the stage,' he explained, 'because there must be some somewhere.' Thus a dramatist must not stage a woman deceiving her husband or a girl being seduced. Only edifying comedies were called for. Meanwhile, the censors in the office of Prefect Dubois would shamelessly mutilate even famous classical tragedies; from Corneille's *Cinna* four lines were struck out in 1803 because they praised the merits of abdication! Another play was vetoed because the author had given the name of Prefect Dubois to a valet. Much of the work of the censor depended on current events; for instance, the banning of an anti-clerical play at the time of the Concordat.

Napoleon himself had no qualms about suppressing a work he did not like – anything with even veiled references to Empire, or Emperor – nor would he hesitate to excise displeasing lines. He would also intervene, frequently, over the number of free tickets the Théâtre Nationale should hand out, telling it that the theatre should be 'popular', 'so that the *people* could enjoy it'. Forcefully, and loudly, he dismissed Shakespeare as so much rubbish: 'I have read him,' he declaimed in front of a full Conseil d'État in February 1803: 'There is nothing which compares to Corneille, or to Racine. There is no way of reading one of his plays, they make one sorry for him ...' Subserviently, the Geoffroy followed up on *Macbeth*: 'This kind of tragedy, very good once upon a time for shocking the rabble of London, doesn't appeal at all to the people of Paris.' *Hamlet* was allowed to play – but only when extensively mutilated.

Taste, always influenced from the top, was on the whole unreceptive to comedy. 'Our comedies serve no purpose [i.e. *political* purpose],' Napoleon once complained: 'On the other side of the Rhine they are not understood.' (The Tsar, however, loathed tragedy to the point of never having one performed in the Russian court.) Beaumarchais's *Barbier de Séville* was widely applauded; Marivaux was just acceptable, and Molière would only be performed 'when there is nothing better'. Parisians would rush to *Le Mariage de Figaro*, though (doubtless under instruction) the dead-hand of Geoffroy would complain of its 'indecent immoralities; the development of the puberty of a young page; the ridiculous fascination of a fat countess for this child who has ceased to be a child; that *crapule* of a noble, even stupider than he is debauched'.

On the other hand, new French 'neo-classic' tragedies often dismayed the foreigner; as a German critic observed of the fastidious monotony of situations and personalities: 'All the French heroes are made on the same model, they all explain in the same way the same sentiments and passions. Who has seen one tragedy has seen the lot.' The great tragic dramatist, Corneille, neglected in the eighteenth century, returned to favour because he was the favourite poet of the Emperor. In his heroic characters Napoleon affected to find a sense of *actualité* – possibly to see himself. In *Horace*, audiences could applaud the glorification of intransigent and wild patriotism; while, in February 1806, in *Semiramis* Mlle Raucourt drew prolonged applause with her two rousing lines:

> He who founds a State alone can keep it.
> One must have a hero worthy of this Empire.

Always there was, perhaps inevitably, a tendency to see current events in the old pieces.

*

Nevertheless, as in the day of Louis XIV – and, indeed, as in many other epochs in the life of the Parisian theatre – it was the *parterre* that continued to wield the most effective powers of censorship in the Age of Napoleon. Out of six new plays produced between the summer of 1811 and December 1812, not one was allowed to succeed, as a consequence of repeated interruptions and barracking. On one occasion, 'twenty hot heads' were recorded as climbing across the orchestra and on to the stage, demanding that Mme Duchesnois replace Mlle George in *Phèdre*. On another occasion, in July 1810, Mlle Hordé, playing Cleopatra (in *Rodogune*) was so interrupted by whistles during a famous monologue that, according to Laborie, 'the poor woman fell in a faint, then after a forced interruption, had the courage to come back to finish her role – courage which this time earned her applause'. Uncontrollable rage broke out when another popular actress, Mlle Mézeray, was replaced because of an accident, with even the police unable to calm the crowd, howling for reimbursement. The *parterre* adored Mlle Bourguin, but was nevertheless given to making impolite allusions to her very liberal private life; in the famous scene with Nero in the third act of *Britannicus*, her line 'Sire, I shall go and swell the ranks of the vestal virgins' brought forth such outrageous bursts of laughter that the poor actress had to take flight behind the scenes, to return a few seconds later, her eyes full of tears, and 'applauded by way of apology'. There was furious grumbling when the *parterre* discovered their favourite top player had been summoned by the Emperor, or even by lowly members of the imperial entourage, to give those out-of-town command performances.

For all his acute interest in the theatre in the abstract, according to the sharp-eyed Mme de Rémusat, Napoleon made 'A mediocre audience, frequently distracted or somnolent', not because of any ignorance of drama on his part, but because 'the great man was too constantly absorbed by the preoccupations of real life to take a consistent interest in imaginary adventures'. Once in the royal box, he could be seen lying full length on a sofa of velvet, arms and legs crossed, while behind him stood his attentive aide, General Comte de Ségur, or the Grand Chamberlain, in full uniform. Only seven weeks after Austerlitz, in January 1806, Napoleon's late arrival at the theatre caused the first scene to be played again; and, as has already been noted, it was frequently his disconcerting habit to call for a change of programme at minimal notice, on one occasion at 2 o'clock in the morning for the same day: '*Britannicus* not *Phèdre* again, if you please, Monsieur Talma!'

Like tycoons at Glyndebourne today, Napoleon enjoyed entertaining his grand peers there, and showing them off. After Jena, it was a Prussian prince taken prisoner, while after Wagram, in December 1809, Napoleon was able to parade no fewer than four subjugated kings in his box. (The next time anything similar was seen was April 1814; but then it was the conquering rulers, when the *Jeunesses de Henri V* was played before the Tsar and the King of Prussia as Napoleon languished in Elba.) There were numerous improvised performances at the Élysées of the Théâtre Nationale.

Then Napoleon decided to build a court theatre in the Tuileries, such as he had seen on his voyages of conquest in palaces of the lesser German sovereigns. Not finished until January 1808, its first performance was a disaster because of a sudden plunge of the thermometer; the first act was disrupted by fits of coughing, and the Emperor, out of pity for the women shivering in their *décolleté* dresses, stopped the play. There were also numerous, and exhausting, command performances with actors ordered away at the shortest notice; in April 1810 alone there were eight presentations summoned at Compiègne during Napoleon's second honeymoon, and another sixteen at Fontainebleau the same autumn.

*

The Age of Napoleon produced two new *vedettes* in the shape of Mlle George (alias Josephine Weimer, 1787–1867), renowned in equal parts for her acting, beauty and fierce temper, and Mlle Duchesnois. They launched into a bitter, and foolish, stage quarrel with each other – providing the *parterre* material for some bitchy doggerel:

> Between the two new actresses
> The wits are divided;
> ... To hear one on the stage
> And get the other in bed.

Only fifteen at her début as Clytemnestra in November 1802, but already physically mature with firm, full breasts, Mlle George stunned Paris, and within a few months she had made her way to Napoleon's bed. On his third visit to the Comédie-Française to watch her perform, as Émilie in Corneille's classic *Cinna*, Napoleon arrived late amid cries of 'Recommencez!' When Mlle George then came to the key line, 'If I could seduce Cinna, I can seduce many others too', the *parterre* exploded with delight, all eyes turned towards Napoleon's box. Later that same night he was to collapse senseless from excess in bed with the new star, as an enraged Josephine flushed him *in flagrante* from the imperial bedchamber.

The redoubtable Mlle George did indeed go on to 'seduce many others' in the Empire *galère* – from Talleyrand to Murat, Lucien and Jérôme Bonaparte, and Wellington. Sadly, in her old age she was reduced to keeping the *chalets de nécessité* (public loos) at the Paris Exposition of 1855. When she died at the ripe age of eighty in 1867, Napoleon III was generous enough to defray the funeral expenses of the star who had so enchanted his uncle and a whole generation of *grognards*.

So heated did the *parterre* become as it divided, like rival soccer fans, in support of the two bitter enemies that, in July

1803, Mlle George fainted in the fourth act of *Phèdre* and had to be carried off the stage. The following month an open fight broke out in the *parterre*, terminating the production of *Phèdre*. By November 1806, peace was finally declared as the two hostile stars agreed to share the spoils, and kissed and made up in what Geoffroy described as 'a pretty good comic scene played by two tragic actresses'.

Then, playing both comedy and tragedy, there was Mme Talma, wife of the great actor François-Joseph Talma; but she tended to over-act. 'In tragedy,' writes Laborie, her voice 'plaintive by choice, seemed monotone and whiny (*larmoyant*) when compared with the so vibrant sensibility of Mlle Duchesnois.' While the troupe was visiting Erfurt in 1808, Napoleon in a rage complained bluntly to her husband that he no longer wanted her in tragic roles; her career languished, and she retired three years later.

Among male actors, François-Joseph Talma (1763–1826) reigned supreme. The son of a Parisian dentist who declined to follow his father's calling, in the first decades of the century Talma created the principal roles in all the famous tragedies of the day. He restored the reputation of tragedy in Paris, making roles seem less artificial; skilful at adapting lines of the classics to contemporary events, he also became a close intimate of Napoleon's. Despite his frequent tirades on the stage against 'tyrants', he was to be seen breakfasting at the Tuileries with Napoleon – the Emperor eating his breakfast off a pedestal table, and longing to gossip about artists and intellectuals, and to trot out his views on his favourite roles. Though Napoleon was personally generous to Talma, giving him a supplementary pension in 1804, Talma never received any title or distinction, and was never made an *Académicien*, in contrast to predecessors.

For all her hatred of Napoleon and the regime, Mme de Staël

was equally 'fanatic' about the genius of Talma; while Chateaubriand declared that 'Without Talma, a part of the marvels of
Corneille and of Racine would remain unknown.' Nevertheless,
even Talma-the-Great could be embarrassed. In 1810, shortly
after Napoleon had divorced Josephine on account of her inabil-
ity to bear him an heir, Talma found himself playing Nero in
Britannicus, who at one point speaks of the sterility and eventual repudiation of Octavia; whereupon the master of the boards
found himself so embarrassed that he babbled the unfortunate
verses. Fortunately, Laborie says, 'The Emperor pretended to be
asleep, and a good number of the court imitated him.' On
another occasion, in 1804, when the *parterre* had its knife into
an unfortunate author, even all Talma's efforts could not prevent
the curtain being rung down before the end. But for posterity it
was his name that personified the Théâtre-Français during the
Napoleonic era, and he who brought the Paris stage back into
honour.

The Paris Opéra also felt the heavy hand of Napoleon's patronage. He was unable to sing in tune, but Josephine could and
loved music – her favourite instrument being the harp. Little
more than two years after the bomb attempt while he was on
his way there – in December 1800, at the first Opéra Ball since
the revolution – there was another minor disaster when the
glass of the chandeliers broke, spraying hot oil over the dresses
of the dancers. But the measure of his interference was about
the same as in the theatre. From his battle headquarters at
Finkenstein in 1806, he wrote to Cambacérès:

> It would be, however, going too far for me to interfere in the
> quarrels of the theatre [but he did!] therefore I charge you exclu-
> sively with the surveillance of the Opéra until my return. I don't
> want to hear any more about it. Let severe discipline reign, and
> make it respect authority.

The following year he wrote to Fouché: 'I am very dissatisfied with the handling of the Opéra. Let Director Bonet know that matters of intrigue will not succeed with me ... If it doesn't cease I will give them *un band militaire* which will make them march with drums beating.'

Immediately on his return to Paris, Napoleon summoned the three curators of the Opéra to ask them what was happening. He had one dancer sent to prison for having, under a poor pretext, refused to dance in front of the Emperor; and the Prefect of Police had no hesitation to imprison a singer who had pretended to have a cold, and would not sing. Just before setting off for Russia in May 1812, Napoleon would demand police intervention against a newspaper that had adversely criticised a new ballet, instructing Savary, 'I would like you to prescribe to journalists more moderation in their articles and more indulgence for an establishment which His Majesty deigns to protect.'

As of 1810, Napoleon ordained, 'You must not put on any new piece without my consent' and 'In general, I don't approve that one should put on any work drawn from the Bible; that should be left for the Church.' Already, in 1800, the usage of certain words in opera had been banned by the censor. *The Magic Flute* was horribly bowdlerised, a sacrilege that passed unnoticed by Parisian critics; *Don Giovanni* was likewise rejigged – with the result that it ran for no more than twenty-eight performances. As for the ballet, Napoleon did not like allegorical ballets, preferring *The Rape of the Sabines*: 'One should only give mythological and historical ballets, never allegorical ones.' On the other hand, a heroic opera like *Le Triomphe de Trajan* by Jean François Lesueur, first shown in October 1807, had a brilliant career, unaffected even by Napoleon's disaster in Russia. Its hundredth performance took place, however, in 1814. Apparently, young officers attending as part of Tsar Alexander's staff had to be prevented from having *Trajan* changed to *Alexandre*.

In 1808, Napoleon's architect, Fontaine, was instructed to draw up 'a fine project' for a new home for the Opéra. It was to be 'a little like that of Milan', no less. Napoleon himself laid down the specifications, but noted somewhat casually that it could be 'located anywhere'. Work on the project, however, did not even begin until 1813, while – during the fifteen years of Napoleon's reign – planning of the new Opéra was put back many times, as the existing one ran up enormous deficits. It would not be completed in all its modern glory until after the fall of his nephew, Napoleon III.

One of the perennial discussions of the novels of Jane Austen is how she could have lived through the whole Napoleonic era, have written so much, but mentioned virtually nothing about the brutal war going on all round. This becomes perhaps a little less remarkable when one considers equally how little life in France was affected by the war, until the Allies arrived there in 1814. What is far more instructive, and indeed puzzling, is how few writers of distinction were thrown up in France at all during the periods of the revolution, the Consulate and the Empire. Yet this was a time when, across the Channel, England was enjoying one of its greatest ages of literature, dominated not only by Jane Austen but also by poetic giants such as Wordsworth, Keats, Shelley, Byron and Coleridge. It was also a time when Schiller, Goethe and Kleist produced their most famed works in Germany. Yet, not a single French play of any value dates from the Napoleonic period.

André Chénier (1762–94), generally held to have been the greatest French poet of the eighteenth century, was guillotined in 1794, two days before the fall of Robespierre. Between him and Lamartine (1790–1869), who only enjoyed his literary career under the Restoration, the *Oxford Book of French Verse* has only three minor poets to offer: Béranger, Millevoye and Valmore. There were poor poets under the Empire, creators of amiable pastiches like Delille and Chênnedollé, who was best known for his friendship with Chateaubriand. Otherwise, for true poetic talent comparable to the great contemporary Romantics of England one has to reach out for a master of prose, Chateaubriand. But together with Chateaubriand, the other founder of the French Romantic tradition, Germaine de Staël, spent most of her working life under the Empire abroad in exile.

For, with perhaps just a passing similarity to the Soviet Union at the peak of its imperial power, one class that was less than impressed by the recompense of 'bread and circuses' in exchange for an authoritarian regime was the intelligentsia. Apart from Chateaubriand and Mme de Staël, notable novelists were almost non-existent. They realised how, having no faith in freedom himself, Napoleon gave minimal support to arts and letters – which always tend to wither in a climate of despotism. A disenchanted Mme de Staël soon found that her France had become 'a garrison where military discipline and boredom rule'.

Perhaps more than from direct political persecution, artists under Napoleon suffered from the restrictive, stifling atmosphere that was produced by a combination of fear, flattery and censorship. Certainly it was in this atmosphere, and in her constant opposition to Napoleon's authoritarian rule, that Mme de Staël, her *salon* having become a focus of the opposition, was forced into exile in Switzerland in 1803, again in 1806 and – definitively – after the seizure of her highly critical *De l'Allemagne*, in 1810. With some courage, she would repeatedly endeavour to return, but would repeatedly be expelled. It was also this atmosphere and its essential lack of liberties which, once their gaze had penetrated the shiny surface of Napoleonic France, gradually disenchanted the liberal visitors from England during the Peace of Amiens, making them think themselves perhaps better off after all in their own backward but libertarian society.

*

If Napoleon's relations with great literary figures of the time like Mme de Staël and Chateaubriand were strained, his dealings with the scientific intelligentsia were much more serene – and deserving of praise. It was not insignificant that, in 1785, he had taken courses at the Académie Militaire from Louis Monge and from the mathematician and astronomer Pierre-Simon de Laplace, whom he appointed briefly as Minister of the Interior during the Consulate, and later made a senator. As a further example of his attraction to men of science, another of his Ministers of the Interior, Jean-Antoine Chaptal, was also a scientist, authorised by Napoleon to endeavour to synthesise politics with industry.

Among chemists, Claude-Louis Berthollet, discoverer of the use of chlorine for bleaching, and one of the founders of the Polytechnique, had accompanied Bonaparte on the expedition to Egypt. (Earlier Bonaparte as a young general had searched Italy for mercury, which Berthollet needed for his researches in Paris.) Afterwards Napoleon helped him to set up a laboratory in Arcueil as an important semi-official centre of scientific research. In 1806, Laplace moved there, while in 1807 Berthollet received a subsidy of ff150,000 from Napoleon, and was also appointed a senator, granted an annual salary of ff22,000 as well as use of the former episcopal palace in Narbonne. Under Napoleon, Arcueil was to have an important influence on the evolution of the École Polytechnique. As a recognition, perhaps, of Napoleon's support, it was the *polytechniciens* who defended Paris staunchly in 1814 and welcomed him back during the Hundred Days in 1815.

Among other scientists equally honoured by Napoleon was Louis XVI's mathematician and astronomer, Joseph-Louis Lagrange, who in his old age was brought back from Berlin by Napoleon, given an important position in the Académie des Sciences, and made senator and Count of the Empire, in 1808. When circumstances of war made it possible, British scientists like Humphrey Davy and John Dalton from the Royal Society derived considerable benefit from the work of their counterparts in France. Robert Fulton, too, the brilliant American inventor of the first submarine prototype, was encouraged (at least initially) by Napoleon. Fortunately, perhaps, for the Royal Navy, he was discouraged by the traditionalist head of the French Navy, Admiral (Denis) Decrès, who scathingly informed him that his invention was 'good for the Algerians', but not France. Fulton then departed for London, where he received similar discouragement. But, altogether, under the Empire science in all its ramifications was accorded the highest privileges and priorities, with enormous strides made by both technology and science under Napoleon.

Yet, for all these advances in science and technology – where clearly Napoleon's interests lay – in the world of the imaginative arts Imperial France remains something of a cultural desert. No new drama, no novels, no poetry or music worth the name – and the visual arts, too, had little of distinction to offer. The elegance of the eighteenth century, the exquisite draftsmanship of Watteau, Fragonard, Greuze and Hubert Robert, all designed to lift the spirits – where had it all gone to? France could mourn its passing, but there would be little of true greatness again until the advent of Delacroix and Géricault with the Restoration.

The Conservatoire des Arts et Métiers was regarded by artists as one of the most useful establishments in the French empire, but combined expositions of 'arts and industry' held in the Louvre provoked reluctance among the artists to show their work under the same roof as craftsmen. So two separate halls had to be constructed. Most of the best French talent, like Ingres – disappointed by cool Parisian reactions to his work – drained off to Italy. Thus the field was largely left open to Jacques-Louis David (1748–1825), the historical painter turned Romantic, who – backed by the Emperor – came to exercise a semi-dictatorship over contemporary French art. Under him it became, according to Maurois, 'imperial, pompous and allegorical'. There was his pupil and protégé, François Gérard, the portraitist commissioned by Bonaparte to decorate Malmaison – and to paint the famous battle triumph of Austerlitz; there was Baron Antoine-Jean Gros, another pupil of David, and equally employed in the glorification of the regime with his massive canvas of Eylau. Depressed in his later years after the fall of the Empire, he drowned himself in 1835. And there was Pierre-Paul Prud'hon, famed for his commissioned portraits of Napoleon and Josephine. But not many others.

David (who, though Delacroix lauded him as 'le père de la peinture moderne', always strikes one as something of a hack) had been court painter to Louis XVI; turned regicide, he was once scathingly described as the 'Raphael of the *sans culottes*'. He found renown for his portrait of Mme Récamier, on her eponymous sofa, and the melodramatic equestrian portrait of Napoleon crossing the Alps. But he was not an easy man, shamelessly ambitious, and greedy; indeed, he was widely known for his *ladrerie* (meanness). It was following the Austerlitz campaign that paintings of Napoleonic victories began to be commissioned. Artists were paid handsomely: David received ff12,000 each for nine big paintings, and ff6,000 for seven smaller. His huge painting of *The Sabines* had already brought him ff72,000, which enabled him to buy a farm in Brie; he then tried to double his profit by reselling the same painting to the Emperor for a further ff72,000. Napoleon, however, angrily riposted with a brusque 'Adjourned'. One state portrait, commissioned for the city of Genoa, and partly executed by one of David's students, in 1806, especially provoked Napoleon's rage:

I have just seen the portrait that David has done of me. It is such a bad portrait, so filled with faults, that I will in no way accept

it. I do not want to send it to any city, especially to Italy where
it would give a bad idea of our school.

Nevertheless, five years later David, thinking the storm had
passed, rashly insisted on demanding a payment of ff10,000;
Napoleon refused. Under pressure from Denon, he haggled over
the payment for the famous coronation picture – from ff100,000
down to ff30,000 – so David painted himself into the scene. But,
despite the liberties taken, Napoleon, on seeing David's vast
canvas unveiled in January 1808, took off his hat and declared,
'David, I salute you!' Still badgering the Emperor for an annual
retainer of ff25,000 in 1810, eventually David killed the golden
goose, finding himself replaced as court portraitist by the famous
Italian sculptor Antonio Canova. Welcomed fulsomely by Napoleon – 'Here is the capital of the arts; you must stay here' –
Canova nevertheless sought every excuse to return to Rome.

As for the art of caricature, none of the ruler or his policies
were permitted, which accounted for the serious dearth in
France of the cartoonist's art, when Gilray and Rowlandson
were at their outrageous peak in England. When the British
Opposition leader, the much caricatured Charles James, visited
Napoleon in the autumn of 1802, and rashly remarked that no
one in England minded being abused in the press, his host
shouted 'It is another thing here!' and strode away. He nevertheless showed an almost morbid fascination with the savage
British cartoons of himself.

8   *The Romantic Image*

What centuries have dimly meditated
His mind surveys in brightest clarity;
All that is petty has evaporated,
Here nothing is of weight save earth and sea.
    Goethe praises Napoleon, 1811

Napoleon had made himself the political and military master of much of Europe. But what, in fact, was the net cultural impact of Napoleon abroad? In short, at least initially, it was rather more than at home – despite the undiminished alarm that Napoleon's dynamism, and the legacy that he had inherited, continued to arouse among his neighbours. The Great Revolution had shaken the whole European dynastic system so fundamentally that it was being excessively optimistic to presume that equilibrium could be restored by the exchange of an island here and a province there. If, in France, Napoleon was most intrinsically both product of the revolution and heir to it, then beyond her frontiers there was also barely a nation whose institutions had not been profoundly affected by the revolution and its consequences.

In Poland, Kościuszko, sparked by what he had experienced in America and observed in France, had launched an abortive insurrection against the Russian oppressor in 1794. In Prussia, where intellectuals like Kant and Hegel, Goethe and Schiller were sharply divided by the revolution, Silesian peasants in 1792 had declined to pay their tithes to their Junker landlords; in Piedmont, Italian peasants had rioted for land reform. In England, radical agitation had spread through Liberal 'Corresponding Societies', although perhaps a more influential phenomenon was the religious revival (especially within the

Nonconformist churches) provoked by outrage at the excesses of French atheism. And in Austria, where the reigning Habsburg had been forced to watch impotently while his sister, Queen Marie-Antoinette, had been first humiliated, then guillotined, there were also dynastic considerations not lightly to be papered over.

To many thinkers and writers in foreign lands at the time, Napoleon appeared – at least initially, and perhaps superficially – as a hero of the Romantic Movement, whereas at home in France it would fail to bloom until late in the nineteenth century. Even in hostile England, in the early days, he found sympathy among liberal Whigs to whom the ideals of the revolution of '89 appealed, and there were chords to be struck among the Romantics. Written far from the realities of war, much of their support, or opposition, amounted to the kind of showbiz posturing familiar to America during the Vietnam War or indeed, more recently, to Britain during the Second Gulf War by opponents of those conflicts. In his book *Napoleon*, Paul Johnson fairly draws a parallel with latter-day Western fans of Mao and Castro, such as Jean-Paul Sartre and Norman Mailer. Attitudes towards Napoleon among British literati tended to be highly personalised and subjective, serving the mood of the moment, mirroring their own prevailing aspirations. Thus they were in love with an image of Napoleon that was partly self-invented. Some of the poets were also very young. Keats wasn't born till the year Napoleon fired off his 'whiff of grapeshot'; Shelley, the year the monarchy fell; while Byron was still at Harrow when the Grande Armée was encamped at Boulogne. Only Wordsworth (b. 1770) and Coleridge (b. 1772) were relatively more mature.

In the early days, at least, Napoleon appealed as embracing the 'human rights' expectations of the revolution – or as an embodiment of the hero 'in an age in which the artist was increasingly seen as heroic,' observes Simon Bainbridge in his excellent book, *Napoleon and English Romanticism*. Keats could damn Napoleon for having done 'more harm to the Life of Liberty than anyone else could have done'; yet he was not beyond adopting him as a symbol. Shelley could rate him as a hero, then as 'Tyrant of the World' (while still at school), and finally damn him for the war in Spain 'where ruin ploughs her gory way'.

Epithets varied between the 'greatest' and the 'meanest'; the list of historic figures with whom Napoleon was compared ran from Alexander the Great, Ulysses, Tamberlaine, etc. down to George Washington. The older and more staid Lakeland poet Wordsworth (already thirty at the time of Marengo) was always fairly consistent in his disapprobation of Napoleon, starting with his driving Liberty from 'Alpine holds' by his invasion of Switzerland in 1798 (though even here there was an element of subjectivity; it impinged on Wordsworth's own idyllic recollections of recent rambles in the Alps). As the war against Napoleon progressed, so Wordsworth became increasingly vehement in his detestation of Napoleon; shocked, particularly, by Napoleon's cruelty to the simple country-dwellers of the countries he invaded, despoiled by France's hungry troops.

> We all are with you now from shore to shore: –
> Ye men of Kent, 'tis victory or death!

he would write defiantly at the time of the invasion threat. In 1804, Wordsworth was writing how the French had

> ... become oppressors in their turn,
> Frenchmen had changed a war of self defence
> For one of conquest, losing sight of all
> Which they had struggled for ...

Then he joined the Grasmere Volunteers (the 'Dads' Army' of its time), having come now to equate Napoleon with Satan – as did Coleridge. This is a nice local example of the process of

Wordsworth's increasing disillusionment with social radicalism, reflected in the subtle amendment he made to each new edition of his early work. To Wordsworth, Waterloo was quite simply an act of 'Almighty God'.

Another loyal patriot to the core, Walter Scott staunchly resisted the allure of Bonapartism; yet he could reflect that, though morally Napoleon was 'far from a good man', 'he was and will remain the greatest man of his time'. Coleridge saw Napoleon's early victories as resulting from 'the enthusiasm which the spirit of freedom inspired'; he could also (so Bainbridge suggests) find inspiration for 'Kubla Khan' from Napoleon's Egyptian adventure – but later would denounce Bonaparte as 'the evil genius of the planet'. After Brumaire in 1779, Southey, taking it personally, would complain 'the Corsican has offended me'; but a matter of weeks later was declaring: 'I do not hesitate in pronouncing him the greatest man that events have called into action since Alexander of Macedon.' On the escape from Elba, in terrible doggerel, Southey, in *The Poet's Pilgrimage*, would then compare it with 'Satan rising from the sulphurous flood'.

In the 1790s, Southey and Coleridge alternately saw Napoleon as a 'genius', 'man of science', 'philosopher', 'poet' and 'peacemaker'. Charles Lamb, partly because of his hatred for the Prince Regent, thought Bonaparte 'a fine fellow'. Similar personal anti-monarchical sympathies caused Walter Savage Landor to go completely overboard, telling his mother that he wished 'the French would invade and insist on hanging George III between two such thieves as the Archbishop of Canterbury and York'. He would praise Napoleon's Egyptian expedition as being 'undertaken on behalf of intellectual cultural progress', while his campaign in Italy signified purely an expansion of 'the spirit of Liberty' beyond France's borders. Then, having visited France in 1802 during the Peace of Amiens, Landor recanted violently, seeing Napoleon as Richard III, the villainous usurper, and writing in robustly chauvinist style: 'Doubtless the government of Bonaparte is the best that can be contrived with Frenchmen. Monkeys must be chained ... As to the cause of liberty, this cursed nation has ruined it for ever.'

In all this it was George Gordon, 6th Baron Byron of Rochdale, who was predictably the maverick, the one who stood alone, deeply subjective and seeing in Napoleon something of his own self-willed, isolated heroes – influenced by Goethe's Werther, who was in turn in thrall to Bonaparte. From having a bust of Napoleon in his room at Harrow, Byron graduated to a lasting identification with him, promoting himself in *Don Juan* (canto XI) as 'the grand Napoleon of the realms of rhyme', in *Childe Harold* (III) as 'the ... greatest of men'. Like his *confrères*, in the early days Byron had responded eagerly to the emotional appeal of the French Revolution, heralding Bonaparte as its *prince-héritier*; on his voyages across Europe, he would travel in an extravagant coach (costing £500, which he could ill afford) modelled on Napoleon's. In common with Hazlitt (and Stendhal), he regarded Napoleon's destruction of the Venetian Republic as 'an act of liberation' – and hoped that he would follow it up to liberate his beloved Greece from the Turks ('useless rascals').

Then followed deep shock at Napoleon's invasion of Spain, and disillusion with his hero's behaviour after Moscow: 'I did not think he would run away from himself.' He despised the Emperor for his spineless abdication in 1814 in 'Ode to Napoleon Bonaparte':

> 'Tis done – but yesterday a King!
>   And arm'd with Kings to strive –
> And now thou art a nameless thing
>   So abject – yet alive!
> Is this the man of thousand thrones,
>   Who strew'd our Earth with hostile bones...

> And can he thus survive?
>   Since, miscall'd the Morning Star
> Nor man nor fiend hath fall'n so far.

But Byron felt Waterloo changed nothing, certainly in the lot of subject peoples, and with it came his deep hatred of the British government and Wellington, his blisteringly savage lines on the suicide of Castlereagh – 'the intellectual eunuch'. In another war, Byron (if in England) would most likely have been imprisoned under Section 18[b].

Then, with yet another turn of the wheel, in a subsequent generation, it was Byron who among the British literati would most influence the later-comer French Romantics of the 1830s.

Finally, in the aftermath of Napoleon, there was Hazlitt (b. 1778), worshipping him as, alternately, the 'greatest man in modern history' or 'the only great man in modern times'. But in his essay on *Legitimacy*, he would freely admit to 'a passionate attachment founded on an abstract idea'. Napoleon 'put his foot upon the neck of kings, who would put their yokes upon the necks of the people', declared republican-minded Hazlitt, mythologising, in his preface to *Political Essays* of 1819. To Hazlitt, in his *Life of Napoleon Buonaparte*, Napoleonic France was 'a citadel in which Freedom has hoisted the flag of revolt against the threat of hereditary servitude'.

In his own time, however, it was in the lands to be invaded by Napoleon that his star burned brightest. Who else but Saxony's Goethe, as late as 1811, could have written:

> What centuries have dimly meditated
> His mind surveys in brightest clarity;
> All that is petty has evaporated,
> Here nothing is of weight save earth and sea.

Napoleon eagerly read 'Werther' in his brief period of intro-spective youth, confiding to his diary, aged seventeen, in a groan of *Weltschmerz*: 'What fury drives me to my own destruction? Indeed, what am I to do in this world?' Werther eventually yields to his despair, rejecting life and killing himself. But this was something Napoleon would never contemplate – at least not until the very end, when Fate seemed to have turned inexorably against him; for, unlike Werther, with Napoleon despair would dissolve the moment he entered the world of action.

Perhaps not surprisingly, in the light of subsequent history, nowhere was Napoleon's influence stronger than among the literati of invaded Germany. Hegel was said to have stood bare-headed in the street, even when the French soldiery stole his possessions; to him, Napoleon represented the 'Embodiment of the Absolute Ideal'. For Goethe, with the famous 'cannonade of Valmy' (which, in 1792 had turned back the Allied armies invading Revolutionary France) there began a new epoch in world history, as the Convention proclaimed its intent to carry the revolution to all the 'oppressed' nations. He saw it all perhaps much as a latter-day Trotsky might have done. In many ways, the Romantic Movement in Germany, with its *Sturm und Drang*, prefigured the violence of the French Revolution. Wasn't much of it, after all, about sexual love, combined with an irrational urge for death?

As Schiller remarked of his fellow Romantics, with their rejection of the prosaic, philistine, commonsense world in which they lived, 'What they admired most was their own emotions; what they despised most was other people's opinions.' It was all not so very far from the fundamental ethos of Napo-leon. In the words of Christopher Herold, Goethe 'with more enthusiasm than accuracy', after the revolution came to see Napoleon, logically, as 'the expression of all that was reasonable, legitimate, and European in the revolutionary movement'.

At Erfurt in 1808, close to his beloved Weimar and even after

Napoleon had invaded, Goethe was delighted to see Talma and the Comédie-Française. Bowing deep, he accepted the Légion d'Honneur from Napoleon, though he declined his invitation to Paris. Five years later, when Napoleon's 'star' had visibly declined and the Battle of the Nations was about to inflict decisive defeat on the Grande Armée, Goethe remained obstinately sceptical about Prussian chances, declaring 'shake or change as you will, the man is too strong for you'.

Not all Europeans remained as enamoured with Napoleon for as long as the genius of Weimar. In Vienna, Beethoven composed a symphony, the *Eroica*, for Napoleon – then, disillusioned with the worldly arrogance of his hero as demonstrated by the coronation of 1804, cancelled his dedication. 'Is he then also nothing more than an ordinary human being?' he lamented to his friend, Ferdinand Ries: 'Now he too will trample on all the rights of men and indulge only in his ambition. He will exalt himself above all the others and become a tyrant.' A remarkable prediction; Beethoven then went to the table, took hold of the title page by the top, tore it in two, and threw it on the floor. What he really felt about the new Emperor was perhaps better demonstrated in his impassioned one-and-only opera, *Fidelio*. A hymn to freedom, fidelity, hope and courage under imprisonment, it first played to empty houses in Vienna, in November 1805, then occupied by the French. Was a disillusioned Beethoven thinking of Napoleon and, possibly, of the brutal execution of d'Enghien that March? Meanwhile, in France that same year, one of Napoleon's chief supporters among the intelligentsia, Chateaubriand, had also resigned in anger after the murder of the duke – then emigrated, and joined forces with Mme de Staël in opposition to Napoleon. In consequence, Napoleon would never bewitch liberal intellectuals at home with anything like the same degree of success that he had had with their counterparts abroad.

*

In Napoleon's France of twenty-seven million, apart from Paris and Lyons no city had a population of 100,000 or more – and Paris numbered well over 500,000. Ever since the *Roi Soleil*, and before, France had become progressively centralised, and under Napoleon it came to assume an even more top-heavy aspect. Yet, even by the latter part of the nineteenth century, two generations after Napoleon, for half the people of France French remained a foreign language. Such was the bad state of the roads that communities were kept apart, their inhabitants forced to live an isolated life, as if in a chemical retort. The kind of life of unrelieved tedium as suffered by Mme Bovary in her Normandy village was probably even more the norm at the time of Napoleon several decades earlier. But the plight of the ruined nobles, who had survived the revolution living in the country-side, making the best of a dull existence in the small plot of land still remaining to them, was particularly dreary. Hospitality was perhaps their one and only luxury; there would be no butler, but still a cook. How much worse was it for those lower down the social scale?

Denizens of Paris were contemptuous of what they found in the provinces; to Stendhal, Dijon and Rouen were each 'an execrable hole, inferior even to Grenoble' – though he confessed a certain indulgence for Marseilles where he had had a few jolly love affairs. After attending a ball in Moulins in 1805, Julie Talma complained: 'I don't think you would find such a sense-less *canaille* [rabble] anywhere but here.' Nevertheless, she noted how the theatre was an important focal point; by 1813 the provinces could boast no fewer than 128 regular theatres – and despite the high fees demanded by visiting stars from Paris.

During the Peace of Amiens, Napoleon had been tireless in his touring of provincial France, to encourage the manufacturers in cities like Lyons, Rouen, Elbeuf and Le Havre, and on many occasions he had presided in person over local meetings to work out the new Civil Code. In this pre-railway age, undoubtedly

Napoleon did much to improve France's highways; but they all tended to radiate out from the hub of Paris, towards strategic frontiers with clear-cut military intentions. There was, for instance, the remarkable engineering feat of the road over the Simplon pass; but that was designed pre-eminently with a view to easing the transport of troops to Italian battlefields. Little was done to use roads to link communities together. When time, and campaigns, permitted, Napoleon would make frequent visits to the provinces. Indeed, a new era had begun with the nomination of prefects by the Consulate, instead of as perks doled out among local grandees. As in Paris, there was substantial reconstruction of old cities like Lyons and Cherbourg – canals were dug, marshes drained and bridges thrown over rivers. The peasant population and the middle classes felt the benefit of all this, but war and the collapse of the Empire was to bring a premature end to all such new development.

Meanwhile, there was another class of men confined to the provinces – these were the English tourists caught in France and interned after the breakdown of the Treaty of Amiens. All those found straggling behind in the pleasure spots of Paris had been rounded up; some had lucky escapes, like the Duke of Argyle, who dressed himself up as a maidservant. But many others were sequestered in the ancient fortress of Verdun. They were treated well, and regarded it as being 'more like a country holiday' – putting on plays in English, and being allowed to make excursions into the surrounding country, with wolf and wild boar hunts. In some contrast was the plight of the French prisoners confined in hulks in Portsmouth, and elsewhere.

9   Decline

For twenty years so many uninterrupted successes made us think reverses impossible.

Mlle Avrillon, keeper of the Empress's jewellery

At Erfurt in 1808, Napoleon had been rather more successful in charming Goethe than Tsar Alexander II, who was still smarting from the defeats of the preceding years, and humiliated by Tilsit. With Russia's commerce suffering acutely from Napoleon's Continental System, which Russia had been forced to accept, it was a matter of time before the reluctant allies would become foes again. For Napoleon, things had begun to go sour since Tilsit and Erfurt, and would grow sourer still with each succeeding year.

In his attempt to break the British naval stranglehold, Napoleon would allow himself to become embroiled in Spain. It was his greatest strategic folly to date; though initially he would chase Sir John Moore all the way across the country, killing him and expelling his 'contemptible little army' from Corunna, and all but expel Wellington from the Iberian Peninsula. It is worth noting that, before 1808, not a single British soldier fought on the European continent. At Waterloo, only 35,000 of Wellington's troops would be English, the other 43,000 German and Dutch. Thus it could be said that Napoleon himself gave Wellington the opportunity to open a vital 'Second Front' in Portugal and Spain. Napoleon would make his inept brother King of Spain, brother-in-law Murat King of Naples, and so on; the conquest of Europe might seem complete, yet on her thrones were only relatives, cronies or time-servers. Like Hitler in the mountains of Yugoslavia in the Second World War, in Spain Napoleon would be defeated by guerrilla warfare and the very brutal living-off-the-land that he himself had invented.

Eventually the 'Spanish Ulcer' cost France a quarter of a million men, soldiers that the Grande Armée could well have used in Russia in 1812. Provoked by his disarray in Spain, Austria would rise up to strike again in 1809; Napoleon would win once more, but Wagram gave him his last victory – and a hard-fought one at that. At the same time that he was endeavouring to conquer all Europe, he was arousing just that popular nationalism which had made the revolutionary France he had inherited so very formidable in the first place.

Meanwhile at home, ever desperate to ensure the permanence of his dynasty, Napoleon had decided to divorce Josephine – since she had proved unable to present him with an heir. He had returned to Paris from Spain in January 1809 to find morale there disquietingly low. The stock exchange was nose-diving once more. Now the superstitious groaned; even the Emperor had admitted that the popular Empress was his guiding 'star'. With sad dignity Josephine accepted her fate, retreating to her beloved Malmaison. To replace her, and supply an heir, Napoleon contracted a marriage with the daughter of his recently defeated enemy, the Emperor of Austria, the nubile nineteen-year-old Grand Duchess Marie Louise. Riding out to meet her cortège at Compiègne, the impatient Emperor, making sure of his deal in the best Mediterranean tradition, bedded her then and there, without waiting for the elaborate state wedding that was to follow.

The grand *entrée* into Paris for Napoleon's second marriage was ominously dogged by misfortune. First, carpenters working on the wooden framework of the full-scale replica of the unfinished Arc de Triomphe went on strike. The Inspector General of Police took a stern line, having six thrown into jail. But an even worse augury for the future followed, at the ball at the Austrian Embassy to celebrate the imperial marriage. As the dancing began, a violent storm sprang up, wafting the curtains on to a cluster of candles. In seconds the ballroom was ablaze, with the hostess, Princess Schwarzenberg, and many others burnt to death. Benjamin Constant's wife Charlotte, who was there, recorded the scene for him:

> I swear that I still think I'm living in a nightmare – a bare seven minutes covered the whole time from the moment we all started for the doors ... the flames reached out into the garden after us ... we heard the big mirrors cracking and the chandeliers crashing down ... and through it the screams of the wretched beings who were still inside.

To add to the disaster, firemen who were rushed to the scene proved to be drunk. It was hardly an auspicious omen for the imperial marriage of Austria and France.

On the day of the wedding, there were various unforeseen hitches and delays which infuriated Napoleon, to the extent that he made Prefect Frochot cut short his circumstantial speech. It was a manifest exaggeration when the official report declared that 'the majority of the population' of Paris had turned out for it. Certainly this was no repeat of the coronation of 1804. Napoleon decided to hold the actual celebration of the marriage, on 2 April 1810, in the main gallery of the Louvre. There Denon had prepared the most lavish of receptions, transforming it hastily into an *ad hoc* chapel. The Salon of 1810 had proved to be the most brilliant of the reign, displaying a multitude of portraits including David's panegyrical *The Distribution of the Eagles*, from which the artist (always eager to please, for a fee) had only just had time to paint out the figure of Josephine. Numerous, too, were the *Images d'Epinal*, all depicting military triumphs. Attempts to move paintings – including *The Marriage at Cana* – to provide space for the new imperial wedding had nearly ended in the destruction of that immense painting, which had been brought from Italy after such a struggle. Napoleon's reaction to this hitch was described by Laborie as a mix between

'the joke of a *mal civilisé* despot and a child spoiled by fortune –
"Oh well, there's nothing left but to burn them!" '

As the culminating triumph of the ceremony, the nuptial
benediction was stage-managed in the *Salon Carré*.

The Emperor's second marriage offered French artists, poetasters
and hacks a great opportunity, not unlike the wedding of Marie-
Antoinette. When the joyous news, swift to follow, got out
that Marie-Louise was pregnant, another nauseating little jingle
made the rounds:

> ... And the fecundity of Alceste
> Is a certain guarantee of a century of happiness.

Though the projected century of bliss was not to be, on the first
hint of the Empress's pregnancy, 5 May 1810, Napoleon in
Antwerp signed a majestic degree that was designed 'to encourage the public benefaction towards poor mothers and place them
under an august and special protection to give the Empress
Louise, our dear and well loved wife, a particular proof of our
affection'.

In July 1810, Napoleon, assured that Marie-Louise was indeed
pregnant, wanted to find out just how many people had signed
up for his charity – which needed a thousand women – and
discovered that only fifty-nine had. Accordingly, a letter from a
courtier to Frochot pronounced: 'His Majesty is demanding
a first list tomorrow. What are we going to do? I would give a
great deal to spend the day in bed with fever!' The decision was
taken to send out the following thoroughly coercive letter:
'In running through the list of subscriptions to the Maternal
Charity, I haven't found your name. I did not want to submit
the list to the eyes of their Majesties without warning you ...
The lists will close 5 August.' It was a kind of moral pressure
that was difficult to resist.

In the night of 20 March 1811, a young Henri Beyle, better

known as Stendhal, currently serving as a clerk at Army GHQ, was abed with his current girlfriend, Angéline Bereyter. They were aroused by the sudden, repeated booming of the cannon: 'We counted up to nineteen, when mad cheering broke out in the streets. We then realised that we had missed the first three salvos ... the cannon went on booming. It was a boy alright ... a young prince had been born. All around us people went wild with joy.' Stendhal continued, totting up, boastfully – in English – statistics of a rather more intimate nature: 'I make that one or two every day, she five, sex [sic] and sometimes *neuf fois*.'

An imperial heir had indeed been produced: Napoleon II, the unhappy and short-lived *l'Aiglon*. His father named him King of Rome, possibly in cynical remembrance of the defunct Holy Roman Empire, which he had liquidated after Austerlitz. Yet France would never bestow upon his mother, the new Empress, the plump Austrian princess, anything like the affection it had felt for the beautiful and elegant Josephine.

At the imposing christening ceremony of the King of Rome that was held in Notre-Dame on 9 June 1811, the vast crowds that turned out are described by Laborie as being 'more curious than enthusiastic'. Napoleon had hoped that the occasion would be first of a sequence of dynastic celebrations; in the event it was to prove to be the last great party of Empire. The illusion did not last long. There was the continuing, wasting war in Spain, and the truce with Austria that victory at Wagram and the dynastic marriage had created seemed altogether too artificial, too ephemeral, too good to last. Morale had only temporarily been raised by these events. By 1810 desertions from the army had risen dramatically to more than a thousand a day. Even though families of recalcitrants were forced to pay a total of ff170 million in fines, there were many ingenious ways of dodging the draft. In the provinces, many was the farmer's son hiding out in a barn and fed in secret.

Nevertheless, for the Napoleonic upper crust the brilliant life of court balls continued. That was where 'all the eligible men were to be found', recorded Ségur. 'The unfortunate young girls', daughters of the handful of *ancien régime* families of Faubourg Saint-Germain still in opposition to Napoleon, 'to whom attendance at the Emperor's Court balls was forbidden because of their parents' prejudice, led a very dull life ... How were the poor girls ever to find husbands?' In honour of Marie Walewska, still lurking in the wings, still enamoured of Napoleon who had ditched her too, Paris danced the mazurka – which had become all the rage. But beneath the glitter there was deep disquiet. The deposed Josephine was greatly missed for her unfailing gaiety, and there was now no one to temper the Emperor's lack of basic humanity. Even his grandiose schemes for the reconstruction of the city had slowed down since 1805. Still the main thoroughfares remained filthy and insalubrious, and time and pressure of events had not enabled him to make any progress in his plans to build a great new city west of the Champs-Élysées. There were signs, also, that the imperial family seemed to be falling apart at the seams, as disputes and divorces took their toll. Moreover, for the first time since 1805, a major economic crisis was blowing up, accompanied by real shortages of food.

Only a few years after recovering from the crisis that had been precipitated by the Banque Récamier collapse, France was once again in economic turmoil. The causes lay in the chaotic legacy of the revolution, the flaws within the imperial system itself, but, most immediately, in the ever-tightening grip of the British blockade and the impact it had on European commerce as a whole.

It is worth noting that England, too, was feeling the pinch by 1808; business prospects were gloomy, with mounds of unsold manufactured goods piling up at the docks.

> The idle merchant on the useless quay,
> Droops o'er the bales no barque may bear away.

wrote Byron in November 1811. Exports to America had fallen to one-fifth of those in 1810, as a result of the blockade and Napoleon's counter-measures. Twenty-six banks had failed, bankrupting many people. Wages had fallen by one-third, and a parliamentary committee revealed that 'distress in the working class was greater than at any previous time'. The harvest had failed, and Luddism had broken out, accompanied by widespread violence that lasted until early February 1812. Bands of men attacked machinery in Nottinghamshire, and it was reckoned that 'General Ned Ludd' was doing more to occupy British troops than Napoleon and his marshals. By the summer of 1812, Wellington was having to send four regiments back from Spain, because of industrial unrest in the north of England. At one point, indeed, the government had to bring 50,000 men to London, to maintain order; a figure that was far greater than the number of British troops that Wellington would have at Waterloo.

The British economy, nevertheless, was rich enough and sound enough to take the strain; France's was not. Within days of rejoicing at the birth of his heir, on 24 March 1811 Napoleon was presented with some unpleasant home truths. Despite his constantly raising the level of taxation, national revenues had run up a deficit of ff50 million. He was forced to pass an Imperial Decree cancelling the arrears of pay owed to the soldiers who had died for him, thereby cheating even the dead. The banks, led by the Banque de France itself, had got themselves enmeshed in a chain reaction of competitive discounting which the weaker brethren could not afford. A first warning came with the fall of the important house of Lubeck, with repercussions all over Europe. According to Mollien, Napoleon's Minister of the Treasury, there were not twelve banks in Paris that remained truly solvent. Over the past four months there had been more than forty business failures.

Part of the trouble, endemically, was a shortage of credit, and too many middlemen chasing too few goods. In the course of merchandising an item of brandy, for instance, over thirty middlemen could be involved, with the result that by the time it reached its final purchaser it had increased by 34 per cent in price. There were intermediaries selling goods they never possessed, without paying, and without delivering. Speculation was rife; Talleyrand, as previously noted, had no compunction about getting involved, and now some of the generals were too; Dupont, for instance, was supposed to have lost ff800,000 in 1810, in the collapse of a business. Much of the speculation concerned illegal goods run through the blockade, despite the draconian penalties applied. In the spring of 1811, a major consignment of contraband muslins and other fabrics was seized in the Rue Le Peletier right in the most elegant centre of Paris.

At the meetings with his domestic underlings and financiers in March 1811, Napoleon flew into a terrible rage at their incompetence:

> When I published my decrees from Berlin and Milan [setting up the Continental System], the whole of England laughed; you mocked me. I however carried on with my own business; I weighed up maturely my situation with England ... Louis XIV, Louis XV had to make peace; for a long time I should have done so also, if I was governing old France; but I have not succeeded a king of France, I have succeeded Charlemagne: this is the continuation of the French Empire. Louis XIV only had Brest, I have the whole coast of Europe. In four years, I shall have a navy; I shall be master of the coasts all the way to Danzig...

It's 'my customs officers,' he continued, 'who will cause the greatest damage to England ... Very soon I shall have enough beet sugar to supply the whole of Europe.' The Banque de France, he insisted, was 'full of money; it doesn't belong to me, but there is not a *sou* in the Banque d'Angleterre'. It was only a matter of time before England would be bankrupt, and he threatened his audience menacingly: 'I warn you, don't play any games with England; you will be caught, sooner or later.'

The browbeaten businessmen present sat there 'subjugated, flattered, intimidated', not entirely believing the Emperor's claims about the economic successes of the 'System'. The following June, 1812, Mollien dared to observe to Napoleon the home-truth that 'Paris seems to have become the public market chosen by England to direct and consume all its transactions of currency'. The following week, driven over the brink by the double-dealing of his ally, Tsar Alexander, with the English arch-enemy, Napoleon re-crossed the Niemen to invade Russia and teach the Tsar a lesson. It was within twenty-four hours of the date that would be chosen by Hitler, 22 June 1941 – with equally disastrous consequences.

Meanwhile, England had become involved in that most foolish of all wars, the War of 1812 against the United States. A conflict in which neither side distinguished itself, it began through American resentment at the Royal Navy's high-handed boarding of neutral ships at sea, and the severe restrictions that the British blockade imposed on the commerce of the independent nation only so recently achieved. Had the Americans been more efficient, they could easily have threatened England's hold on Canada; in which event, the Duke of Wellington (already under orders to do so in 1814) would almost certainly have been sent to North America and thus would not have been available for Waterloo the following June – with consequences requiring little imagination. Previously, in 1803, Napoleon had gained much goodwill in America by his bargain sale of the vast territory of Louisiana for the trifling sum of $15 million. Now, in 1812, he could well have turned it to his advantage, but he failed. Like another European dictator in 1941, his eyes were fixed solely on Russia...

Even more serious than the renewed financial crisis was the *disette*, or famine, of 1811–12. Initially the harvest of 1811 promised to be excellent; then repeated thunderstorms caused damage. Administrators were caught out because they had foolishly allowed surpluses to run down. In Paris, the first sign, not experienced since revolutionary days, was the sudden increase in the price of rice and vegetables. Between 1811 and 1813, Napoleon summoned no fewer than fourteen meetings exclusively dealing with food supplies, passing decrees that were all too reminiscent of the revolution. By the start of 1812 the price of bread was beginning to spiral. A sack of flour fetching ff93 in February (already an exceptional price) reached ff115 by April. With the bakers of Rouen selling their bread at four times the price of 1803, there were riots in the provinces – with less trouble in the cities only because of the black market and Fouché's ever-watchful secret police. With the introduction of anti-hoarding measures, anxiety was turning to terror as Napoleon was about to leave for Russia. On 3 May, he held an emergency meeting at Saint-Cloud – literally on the eve of his departure. Reserves of grain had all but run out.

On 23 June, the very day he crossed the Niemen into Russia, Étienne-Denis Pasquier, Dubois's successor at the Prefecture of Police, admitted: 'For the last three or four days there has been a kind of a crisis very hard to resolve.' There was a further rise in the price of bread; in human memory, it had never risen so high. Prospects for the winter of 1812 looked grim – and especially for the poor. To distract the hungry and discontented, it provided an additional motivation for Napoleon's assault on Russia. Then, fortunately for Napoleon, and with the kind of luck that was only beginning to desert his 'star', the harvest of

1812 turned out well. Nevertheless, he should have read the warnings already in 1810, and by now he was enmeshed in his first decisive military reverse. In January 1813, the 'reserve' made its last distribution of flour to the bakers. Then a very abundant harvest that summer finally brought back a completely normal situation. The price of bread fell nearly 15 per cent – just in time to counterbalance, for a while, the sombre news of decisive defeat at Leipzig that was coming in from Germany.

Yet it was impossible for Napoleon to ignore the intensity and length of the hardship that the *disette* had imposed. As the fateful 1812 campaign got under way, there was also a limit to how long the French nation, drawing on its revolutionary capital, could go on glorifying war for its own sake. Outside the army itself, always devoted to Napoleon, there was now little enough love for him in the country at large. Increasingly he had to rely on the terror of the ubiquitous secret police, headed since 1810 by Fouché's even more thorough successor, General Savary, Duke of Rovigo, the kidnapper and executioner of the Duc d'Enghien. Soon after assuming office in Paris, Savary had imposed his stamp by executing two clerks in the Ministry of War, shot for passing information to the Russians.

As the Grande Armée headed for Moscow, Paris, recorded Laure, the fun-loving wife of General Junot: 'presented a curious but melancholy spectacle. Husbands, sons, brothers and lovers were departing to join the army; while wives, mothers, sisters and mistresses, either remained at home to weep, or sought amusement in Italy, Switzerland or the various watering-places of France'. Laure herself took off to find distraction with a new lover at Aix-les-Bains, as her husband, the general, became increasingly demented, fighting for his life in the wastes of Russia.

In Paris there continued, nevertheless, the usual circuses to distract Parisians from what was happening to the Grande Armée.

By 1815 Gérard, the famous portraitist, had delivered fifty full-length portraits and forty of bust size. In 1810, Canova returned to Paris. His portrait of Empress Marie-Louise managed to make the young wife appear even younger than she was, and it was suggested that the bust should be mounted on an allegorical base on the Concorde. He projected a vast nude statue of the Emperor, twelve feet tall, in a Greek style. Napoleon's displeasure with it was followed by Canova's fall from favour. His pride cruelly wounded, Canova's massive statue was eventually to end up in the hands of Napoleon's conqueror, Wellington, and it now sits in Apsley House. (The episode of the Napoleon statue set Canova against Napoleon. Personal resentments made him accept a papal mission to go a third time to France to claim back the pictures looted by Napoleon and Denon.)

The periodic exhibitions of current works of art went on in Paris unaffected by the course of war. The Salon of 1810, coinciding with the apogée of the Empire, exhibited a multitude of portraits, notably of the imperial family. An irreverent jingle, composed in 1801, was repeated for the Salon of 1810:

> In the salon where Poussin
> Dazzled with divine beauties,
> I see my uncle, my cousin,
> I see my neighbours, my *voisines* ...

The Empire's last Salon, opening in the Louvre during the course of the retreat from Russia, managed to be the most ambitious yet. No fewer than 1353 works were exhibited, compared with a mere 542 in 1800. Among the first exhibitors there was Théodore Géricault.

Just before Christmas 1812, abandoned by her lover, Laure Junot unsuccessfully took an overdose of laudanum. Then Junot, once the dashing, handsome young Governor of Paris, returned from Russia. *La Tempête* had become 'a coarsened, aged man, walking with difficulty, bent and supported with a stick, dressed care-lessly in a shabby greatcoat', his mind destroyed by war. Thus were its realities slowly coming home to the fun-loving capital, as the mood darkened. One is reminded, more recently, of Berlin as the Soviet colossus began to close in on the city in 1944–5. In the words of Mlle Avrillon, who was in charge of Empress Marie-Louise's jewellery, 'we were all the more terrified … because for twenty years so many uninterrupted successes made us think reverses impossible'.

Mon dieu ... Cossacks in the Rue Racine!
Mme de Staël hears news from Paris

To Talleyrand, out of office and under a cloud, news of Napoleon's defeat at Borodino marked 'the beginning of the end', and he felt 'the end itself could not be far distant'. Though it had been swiftly crushed by Savary's secret police, already while Napoleon was away in Moscow there had been a warning in the shape of an abortive rising by one of his disaffected generals. As soon as Napoleon showed himself back in Paris, however, in the words of Duff Cooper, 'Once more and for the last time treason hung its head, criticism sank to a whisper, and conspiracy crept underground.' Nevertheless, Moscow was to prove but the first stop on the road to St Helena, now inescapably embarked upon.

By the spring of 1813 the vengeful Russians, pursuing Napoleon, entered Prussian territory, threatening the German states still allied to him. Marie Walewska's Poland disappeared once again into the Tsarist maw, while the defeated Germans saw their opportunity to launch into a war of liberation, known as the Battle of the Nations. Napoleon had brought it on himself, in 1806 by sweeping away the old political structure of the German states, and in 1807 by his foolishly harsh treatment of proud Prussia. Leaving her territorially truncated, he made her the leader in the eventual uprising against him. Added to this was the brutal policy of the Grande Armée, living off the land in the German territories they marched through, whether allies or conquered. The genie of German nationalism was well and truly let out of the bottle, and it would come to plague future generations of French, and Europeans.

Despite the disaster of 1812 in Russia, by scraping the barrel Napoleon was still able to find loyal Frenchmen willing to die for him, and even recruit from his remaining European allies. Once more he raised a new army, 700,000 strong. But, in the summer of 1813, for the first time he found himself having to confront simultaneously the armies of Russia, Austria and Prussia, with Wellington in the West grinding forward relentlessly towards the Pyrenees. In October he suffered a decisive defeat at Leipzig, the bloodiest battle of all the Napoleonic Wars, where a total of nearly 100,000 men fell. The writing was now truly on the wall for Napoleon, as the triumphant Allies closed in remorselessly on France itself – for the first time since 1793.

The following spring, 1814, Napoleon fought one of his most brilliant campaigns, rallying his tattered forces with the rousing Cry of 'La Patrie en Danger!' By March he was cornered in Paris, and sought refuge at Fontainebleau. Meanwhile Paris experienced all the horrors and terrors of occupation, though nothing was to compare to the four years of humiliation she would suffer in 1940.

Russian troops entered through the east of Paris, carrying on their third assault the fortified redoubt that brave students of the Polytechnique had run up among the tombs of Père Lachaise. Empress Marie-Louise abandoned Napoleon, returning home to Vienna with the crown diamonds, worth some ff18 million – possibly a reasonable return for all that the Habsburgs had suffered. As she took Napoleon's son and heir with her too, the little King of Rome screamed: 'I don't want to go away!'

On 30 March, Paris came under the first cannon-fire: 'Only the roar of the cannon and the sight of peasants who had fled to the suburbs with their families, belongings and domestic animals, overcame the general disbelief,' wrote an observer, the

Duc de Broglie, incredulous that things could have come to this; that *la ville lumière* could actually be subjected to the fate Napoleon had meted out to other European capitals. Wounded men dragged themselves towards hospitals, unaided by the Parisian populace. Lunatics were driven out of asylums by the army to make way for the hordes of wounded. Refugees from the country hurried in pell-mell with their cows, their sheep and their scanty baggage, cursing the severity of Napoleon's conscription. Close on their heels came the Prussian cavalry and Russian infantry – 'like a merciless dark tide of green uniforms and bright plumes', on a day of superb weather. They were said to know only two words of French, 'brûler Paris'. Yet somehow defeat went hand in hand with a sense of deliverance for the Parisians. In a sudden change of mood, cries were heard of 'À bas le Corse ... Vive notre libérateur.' Orders by Napoleon to blow up the main Paris powder store were fortunately disobeyed.

A frozen Joseph Bonaparte, together with brother Jérôme (both now minus a throne) watched the initial battle from the Heights of Montmartre. Joseph then sneaked out of the city, heading south amid a long line of refugees. It was a scene that would be repeated three more times over the next 126 years. Up at Montmartre, it was reported that the miller of the Moulin de la Galette – together with his brother – had been shot by the Russians, his body then bound to one of the sails of the famous windmill.

Cossacks clattered down the Champs-Élysées, and then encamped there – the first time since the Hundred Years War that a foreign army had entered the proud city. '*Mon Dieu!* Cossacks in the Rue Racine!' exclaimed Mme de Staël from the safety of her Swiss retreat at Coppet. Their behaviour was far from immaculate – but, after what Moscow had suffered, it was surprising that it was not far worse. Talleyrand affected to leave Paris, so that, in the words of his biographer, Duff Cooper, 'He could say that he had endeavoured to do his duty, but had been prevented by force.'

On 6 April 1814 Napoleon abdicated, having ill-advisedly refused Allied terms which might have allowed France to retain the frontiers of 1793. On the 28th he was dispatched aboard HMS *Undaunted* for Elba, the Allies thereby (in the words of André Maurois) 'bestowing on Caesar the kingdom of Sancha Panza'. Europe breathed a sigh of relief, though it was a temporary exile that would last less than a year. Many Parisians turned out to welcome the return of an obese Louis XVIII, his court transported in imperial carriages hastily painted over with Bourbon colours, passing corpses of soldiers being buried in haste. A fortnight after Empress Marie-Louise's precipitate departure, the Comte d'Artois, future Charles X, was sleeping in the Tuileries.

Parisians were reported to be showing 'a very agreeable and polite restraint' towards the Allied troops. The Tsar arrived, cheered at the opera – when accompanied by King Louis and the indestructible Talleyrand – by shouts of 'Vive Alexandre!' that resounded for over half an hour. He was often seen strolling in leisurely fashion through Paris, or taking ex-Empress Josephine for drives in his carriage. (Tragically, contracting pneumonia, she died following one such open-air drive in 1814.) Austria's Prince Metternich, come to make a peace treaty, was greeted with similar enthusiasm. In August Paris took to the streets for a five-day celebration of the Fête of St Louis; as in 1802, once again curious English tourists flooded into Paris:

> London now is out of town
> Who in England tarries?
> Who can bear to linger there?
> When all the world's in Paris?

ran a contemporary jingle. They were astonished at the light-headedness of the Parisians, seemingly indifferent to events. In sharp contrast to the capital, however, was the stark impoverishment of the French ports and countryside. Walter Scott for one was deeply shocked by the ruined homesteads he saw.

Notable *émigrés* returned, like Chateaubriand and Mme de Staël. Now somewhat aged, always wearing a turban and displaying large areas of dilapidated flesh, de Staël set up a salon in the Rue de Grenelle, where she damned Bonapartists and royalists alike. Pozzo di Borgo, who had come to Paris from Corsica as a radical young deputy in 1792, observed the 'new' Parisians and the way 'they watch, judge and tear each other to pieces ... like a play by Beaumarchais'. Everyone, '*without a single exception* is discontented'. It was not exactly a good omen for the future. Amid this the occupying Allies were popular, momentarily, like Americans in 1944. There would be cries of *Vivent les Russes!* but fairly soon they were once again 'the barbarians of the North'. The visiting English, returning after a dozen years' absence, found Paris down at heel, but the boulevards, theatres, cafés, the Palais-Royal, the Louvre, all remarkably little changed. It was to many still, quite simply, 'the most interesting place on earth' – and it was cheap. But also, by early 1815, it had become so unsafe (a cause being the vast numbers of unemployed and penniless veterans) that even the Tuileries were kept lit up all night.

To the returning English it might well have seemed that Parisians were setting eyes on their beloved monarch for the first time, and that Napoleon had never existed. 'People speak of him,' wrote Metternich, 'as if he had ruled in the fourteenth century. All the eagles have disappeared. There are no more of those innumerable Ns ... Everything is as peaceful as if there had been no war ...' There were white cockades and fleurs-de-lis (symbols of the Bourbons) everywhere. But disillusion would follow with astonishing rapidity; vicious caricatures of Louis's obesity would appear as he proved Talleyrand's adage about the Bourbons having 'learnt nothing, and forgotten nothing'. The economy sagged, and inflation took over. The army was shabbily treated, as the streets of Paris swarmed with discharged and unemployed veterans of the Grande Armée. Some 12,000 ex-officers on half-pay took to meeting in cafés, lamenting the 'good old days' of the Empire and conspiring for the Emperor's return.

Fretting on his tiny prison 'empire' of Elba, Napoleon learned that Louis was refusing to pay his pension, and that there was talk about transferring him to a more remote island. One day his unfortunate 'guardian' on Elba, Colonel Sir Neil Campbell, was visiting a mistress in Florence, and Napoleon slipped away aboard a French brig, *L'Inconstant*. On 1 March, accompanied by a thousand men, he landed in the Golfe Juan near Cannes, and began marching swiftly upon Paris, collecting supporters as he went in the most remarkable fashion. In Paris a shaky King Louis told an aide: 'It is revolution once more.'

There now began the miraculous Hundred Days, 'the episode in his adventurer's life which came nearest to pure adventure story', in the words of Napoleon's critical biographer, Correlli Barnett. A brief daily report on Napoleon's progress was provided by the government newspaper, *Le Moniteur Universel*, calling Frenchmen of goodwill to resist:

> L'anthropophage est sorti de son repaire.

Then subsequent headlines:

> L'ogre de Corse vient de débarquer au Golfe Juan.
> Le tigre est arrivé à Gap.
> Le monstre a couché à Grenoble.
> Le tyran a traversé Lyon.
> L'usurpateur a été vu à soixante lieues de la capitale.
> Buonaparte s'avance à grands pas – mais il n'entrera jamais
>   dans Paris.

Amazingly, the tone began to change:

> Napoleon sera demain sous nos remparts.
> L'Empereur est arrivé à Fontainebleau.

and, finally,

> Sa Majesté Impériale et Royale a fait hier au soir son entrée dans
> son château des Tuileries au milieu de ses fidèles sujets.

When the 'ogre' reached Paris, against all calculations, there took place yet another of those astonishing *volte-faces* that occur through French history, and which amazed even Napoleon himself. 'They let me come back just as easily as they let the others go!' he exclaimed. Paris remained remarkably placid, accepting a change of regime in the provinces without concern. The Duc de Broglie noted scathingly in his memoirs,

> Government and society presented an abject picture. False news was exchanged without anyone believing any of it. Passions were roused by speeches that anyone could see through. Everyone prepared for resistance while firmly resolving to avoid any confrontation. All proclaimed their hatred for the tyrant while secretly making their own arrangements.

About the worst upheaval was that, in the Sorbonne, no exams were set that winter and spring.

Meanwhile in the Tuileries Palace, the seamstresses who had been busy unpicking the Napoleonic bees from the carpets, and replacing them with hastily sewn-on fleurs-de-lis, started putting them back as the portly king hastened to leave his kingdom for the second time. Not everybody, however, was happy about the return of the ex-Emperor: in the Tuileries gardens, two men who cried 'Vive Bonaparte!' following Napoleon's escape from Elba were set upon and murdered by women walkers, *à coups de parapluies*, as it has been called. Fouché had to escape possible lynching by jumping over a garden wall, to prepare himself for his next *volte-face* and greet his former master. A typical Parisian quip made the rounds of the poorer districts: 'Why is bread dearer and meat cheaper since 20 March? ... because the baker has left and the butcher has returned.'

But there were others who adapted themselves with similar mobility to the dreadful Fouché. One was Benjamin Constant, liberal novelist and one-time lover of Germaine de Staël, declared foe of Bonapartism. On 19 March he was writing a tract damning Napoleon as Attila and Genghis Khan, and praising Louis XVIII as a friend of liberty. The following day he fled Paris; on the 28th, his action belying his name, he returned to offer his services to Fouché. By 20 April he had been nominated to Napoleon's Council of State. Aged forty-eight, Constant had finally made it. Napoleon himself was scathing about such dexterity: 'They are cowards who change their sovereign as they change their shirt,' he observed to his sister-in-law Julie, the ex-Queen of Spain.

As the Allies began to mass in Belgium, at remarkable speed and with a view to marching once again on Paris, Napoleon's former staff 'calmly and quietly' resumed their duties, except for the generals who, wanting no more Napoleonic adventures, had defected. It was as if Napoleon had returned from 'only a short journey', commented Alexandre Laborde, currently serving on the Paris National Guard. On a forebodingly cold day in May, Napoleon reviewed his swiftly reconstituted new armies on the Champ-de-Mars. There were ripples of scornful laughter at the sight of Cambacérès mincing on to the platform in his new blue cloak spotted with gold leaves – but much apprehension at what lay ahead. It must have seemed, to Parisians, like a long hundred days as Napoleon then set off to meet his fate at Waterloo. The rest, as they say, is history...

In the immediate aftermath of the great battle, false rumours about victory percolated to Paris. Then came the tattered relics of the once-proud Grande Armée with their true, eye-witness accounts of what had happened. The Place Vendôme was covered with wounded soldiers lying on straw. They received little care from a populace apprehensive at what was to come. A visiting Englishwoman, Helen Williams, remarked on how one dying soldier drew 'no tender tear from any female spectator – no interest but that of simple curiosity'. France had become simply too inured to the horrors of war. Paris prepared for siege, but it was only a gesture.

Then entered the conquerors, this time an enraged Blücher leaving a 'desolate path' of destruction all the way from Waterloo to Paris. Determined to wipe out the dreadful slight to Prussians at Jena, he intended to destroy Napoleon's eponymous bridge; only Wellington forestalled him by posting British sentries to guard it (British forces controlled the right bank, Prussians the left). At one moment in the occupation, Prussian cannons were actually trained on the Tuileries Palace. In contrast to the less bitter mood of the occupation of 1814, there were frequent brawls and duels – chiefly between the French and the hated Prussians, more than any other occupying army. 'Occupation costs' were levied at a rate ten times that of the previous year. Swaggering parades, painful to French national pride, were held on the Champ-de-Mars, where only a couple of months previously Napoleon had reviewed the armies that were intended to sweep the Allies out of Belgium. 'The Bois de Boulogne was laid bare,' recalled one Parisian eyewitness, Dr de la Sibouti: 'the statues of the Luxembourg mutilated with sabre cuts; our hearths and homes were overrun by soldiers who spoke to us as masters. Such are the rites of war . . .' Nevertheless, generously, he added: 'Our own soldiers have probably abused them on more than one occasion.'

Certainly compared with the Russian rape of conquered Berlin in 1945, the depredations of the Allies were extremely restrained. But these were more civilised times; for all the damage he had wreaked across Europe, Napoleon had been no Hitler, and warfare of the nineteenth century was a gentler and more humane affair than the genocidal struggles of the twentieth.

Reactions to this ultimate defeat varied across France, and across social strata. Pierre Fontaine, Napoleon's official architect and one who had thus spent many hours with him replanning Paris, noted three days after Waterloo how, abandoning his army once more in defeat: 'He came back to Paris like a fugitive, thinking only of his person ... the magic is gone. We can no longer regard him as someone extraordinary.' Byron's friend, John Cam Hobhouse, arriving a week later, noted 'extravagant rejoicing', while Captain Mercer of the Royal Horse Guards thought it strange that the French were so happy in their defeat.

On 25 June, a schoolboy in Limoges recorded how he and his ardent Bonapartist fellow-students 'were plunged all at once into the deepest dejection. Complete silence reigned in the courtyard.' Yet elsewhere in Limoges people were burning effigies of Napoleon, as Rouen had burned Joan of Arc. Three weeks after Waterloo, Parisians could bring themselves to cheer the victor, the Duke of Wellington; Napoleon's former court painter, the contentious David, moved to Brussels along with many former Bonapartists; Constant, who had a unit of British horses stabled in his house, walked around 'looking like someone condemned to death' (though, remarks Philip Mansel, probably as much on account of his unrequited love for Mme Récamier as the Emperor's defeat).

On 21 June, having abandoned his army for the third and last time, Napoleon summoned Marie Walewska and their son Alexandre to say farewell. 'The mood was lugubrious,' recorded an aide: 'It was raining, the Emperor was burning state papers, and I was packing his personal effects.' The next day he abdicated for a second time. He then headed for Rochefort, in a final delusion that his implacable enemy at Waterloo might either grant him asylum in some comfortable country house in England, or else let him follow other 'asylum seekers' to the USA, to Boston or New York. But they had other plans for the man who had wrecked the peace of Europe over the past twenty years, and on 15 July 1815 he boarded HMS *Bellerophon* for St Helena – 'the ugliest and most dismal rock conceivable', in the opinion of a British surgeon aboard.

As Napoleon's empire unravelled, and France slowly came back to life, his enemies, led by Metternich and Castlereagh – and the inevitable Talleyrand, now representing the new regime, the returned Bourbons – went to work in Vienna to prepare a lasting peace treaty. Though considerably harsher than what was on offer the previous year, they were still extremely generous, by twentieth-century standards. For all his sins, Napoleon had been no Hitler – not a war criminal. Signed in November 1815, the treaty permitted France to keep most of her traditional frontiers, except for the new, neutral Belgium; Savoy handed over to Sardinia, and the German-speaking Saar to Prussia (which signified the beginning of a Teutonic presence on the Left Bank of the Rhine). With the return of Louis XVIII, France was allowed to return, politically, to a *status quo ante*. As reparations she was required to pay ff700 million in gold, but this was eventually whittled down to ff265 million. Compared with the savage reparations that would be demanded by the victors in 1871 and 1919, France escaped lightly in financial terms. The Allies withdrew from Paris swiftly. Much more painful, however, and more difficult to make good, were the losses in dead from the wars of the past twenty years, with estimates ranging from 430,000 to 2,600,000 – almost certainly well over one million – for France alone, out of a total population of 33 million.

1815 and 1816 were bad years for France. There was hunger and deprivation, and over parts of the countryside a 'White

Terror', comparable to the *épuration* that was to follow the Liberation of 1944, held sway. Bands of royalist carpetbaggers looted and settled old scores. In Nîmes Protestant women were beaten because of their religion. Marshal Ney – 'bravest of the brave' – was executed, *pour décourager les autres*, and the heads of several other Napoleonic generals followed suit. But others survived to find places of honour and importance under the new regime; one of the least deserving, Bernadotte, was to become King of Sweden, no less.

With nothing like what Germany and Japan were subjected to in 1945 – no 'de-Napoleonisation' imposed by victorious Allies determined to raze totally an evil system, and start again – French society swiftly repaired itself. Above all, France was allowed to keep the remarkable system, the *Code*, which it had inherited from Napoleon.

With its renowned capacity for recuperation, Paris was soon back to at least a semblance of its former glory. Hardly had the Place Vendôme been cleared of the wounded from Waterloo than chic women were showing off their finest silks there. Government stocks began to take off, and visiting tourists were soon finding Parisian society again milling about in the Tuileries Gardens. Walter Scott described the Palais-Royal, as before, as 'this focus of vice and treason' and a 'central pit of Acheron'; while within a few weeks of Waterloo, Véry Frères' legendary restaurant, where Napoleon's generals had once dined, was filled with English and Prussian officers. Wellington too was seen dining there, in the company of Metternich, while he wasted no time in taking over one of the fallen Emperor's mistresses. Of the plethora of British ambling in the Bois, the Marquise de Coigny remarked: 'It is so like a *fête* that it's a pity it's a conquest!'

If there was one dark hole on the otherwise bravely bright escutcheon of post-Waterloo Paris, it was the fate of the Louvre.

Canova, who (it will be recalled) had been a reluctant visitor to Paris in 1810, when he had sculpted the immense nude of the Emperor, now returned as emissary of the Vatican (paid by London) to recover the looted works of art from 'this great cavern of stolen goods'. Andrew Robertson, the Scottish miniaturist whose visit to Paris coincided with Canova's, was deeply shocked by the emptiness of the Louvre, with its pictures taken away. Sir Walter Scott, writing to his sister at about the same time (July 1815), recorded mounting French rage over the removal of the Louvre paintings: '[French] attachment to these paintings and statues, or rather to the national glory which they conceive them to illustrate, is as excessive as if the Apollo and Venus were still objects of actual adoration.' Wellington had to station his soldiers the length and breadth of the Louvre, amid noisy cries of 'Down with the English'.

As the removals from the Louvre continued, and the oxen carts plodded their weary way back to Rome, Andrew Robertson noted 'a terrible scene of confusion, one division of the room almost entirely naked – the large works of Rubens being taken down made a dreadful blank on the wall ... the people in a rage' and later: 'Paris is in a ferment about these pictures, and the review tomorrow of the whole army under Lord Wellington is a very prudent measure.' By October, he was describing the Louvre as 'truly doleful to look at now, all the best statues are gone, and half the rest, the place full of dust, ropes, triangles, and pulleys, with boards, rollers etc.'

Faced with the inexorable dismantling of all he had achieved in the name of Napoleon, his life's work, Vivant Denon resigned. He died heart-broken in 1825, four years after his master, gazing out from his Left Bank house on the Quai Voltaire at his precious, ransacked Louvre across the Seine. Meanwhile, Canova found he was virtually ostracised by the Paris art world as fellow artists like Gros and Houdon cut him dead. But, worse than that, he found himself living in sheer *timore*, often afraid to go to his lodging there for fear of being murdered; one day, one of the French artists said in his hearing that he should like to stick a dagger into him.

Denon, however, predicted in a letter to Talleyrand of September 1815, 'We have already had some big losses, Monseigneur, but, with time, one could hope to recoup them. The gaps that exist will be filled in the long term.' He was right: almost half of the 506 pictures removed from Italy still hang in French museums. Already by 1816, King Louis was able to exclaim after a tour of the Louvre, 'Allons, nous sommes encore riches!'

In the agreeably chauvinistic little clerihew of E. P. Benson,

> It was not Napoleon
> Who founded the Ashmolean.
> He hardly had a chance,
> Living mainly in France.

Nevertheless, during his stay in occupied Paris, Canova somehow found time to produce his *Ideal Heads*, while the scrupulous English were to pay the French government the handsome sum of £35,000 for his *Napoleon as Mars* – as a nostalgic gift to the Duke of Wellington. Finally, also among the looted treasures wending their way back to Italy, and possibly the cruellest blow to the Parisians, were the famous and much beloved Byzantine horses that Napoleon had installed atop the Arc du Carrousel; these found their rightful home once more above the portico of St Mark's in Venice.

By the close of 1815, the most appropriate of the monuments left in Paris to recall the fallen Emperor was the decaying elephant of wood and painted plaster, standing forgotten by the Bastille. Under the Parisian weather it gradually disintegrated, becoming the home of thousands of rats – and of Victor Hugo's urchin, Gavroche. Seeing it thirty years later, Hugo, who hated all

Bonapartes, latched on to the decrepit mammoth for a passage in *Les Miserables*:

> in this deserted and exposed corner of the Place, the large head of the colossus, its trunk, its tusks, its tower, its enormous rump, its four feet resembling columns, under a starlit night formed a frightening and terrible silhouette ... It was sombre, enigmatic, and immense. It was some kind of potent phantom, visible and upright alongside the invisible spectre of the Bastille.

It also seemed somehow to set the seal on the decay of Napoleonic empire, and all its pomp and circumstance.

Epilogue: End of an Age

If you have not lived through 1815, you do not know what hatred is...

Maurois

I have sealed the chasm of anarchy and I have unravelled chaos.

Napoleon

The age has lost its greatest man. He was far away from our eyes and our thoughts; but we felt a pervading consciousness that he lived and something of a feeling he might again appear among us.

The Examiner, **on Napoleon's death in 1821**

So, *en principe*, the Age of Napoleon ended. But of course it didn't. The age, the legend, continued long after Napoleon's own lonely death on the gloomy mist-bound island of St Helena. 'If I happen to be killed,' Napoleon had declared glumly in the desperate year of 1814, 'my inheritance will not devolve upon the King of Rome. As matters stand only a Bourbon can succeed me.' Whether or not he was in fact killed, as some historians claim today, it remained a remarkable prophecy. The heir Napoleon had so ardently sought would never succeed him; instead he spent the rest of his sad, short life as a virtual prisoner of his Austrian grandfather, with his mother in Vienna.

On 6 July, King Louis XVIII made his formal re-entry into the capital which had twice thrown him out (*Louis deux-fois-neuf* the wags called him). That day Chateaubriand, returning from exile with Louis, witnessed those adept time-servers, Talleyrand and Fouché, welcome him at Saint-Denis, arm in arm, giving rise to his devastating remark about 'Vice Supported by Crime'. Wellington – amazed by the wild cheering – wondered whether it could possibly be the same Parisians who had also cheered Napoleon and then himself in such rapid succession? Altogether, it was hardly the most auspicious beginning to France's decisive return to legitimacy, to the *ancien régime*. 'In June 1815,' wrote French historian André Maurois in eloquent terms:

> many Frenchmen hated Napoleon because they blamed him for the country's losses and defeats; very soon, thanks to distance, to the dislike of the Bourbons, to the resentment against the English, to great memories and the greatness of things recounted about his captivity, hate would give place to pity and then to regret...

As for the army that had followed him so loyally, through so many bloody campaigns, it would 'never cease to recall the small hat and the grey-frock-coat behind which it had "crossed the Alps and the Rhine", conquered all the kings of Europe and carried the tricolour as far as Moscow'. Though he might be deposed, it was Napoleon's shadow that, in 1830, would sweep out the Bourbons once and for all.

As of summer 1815, however, none of this could be foreseen. Politically, there were hopes that Britain might become the model for France's future; but this was not to be. Returning to Paris during the Restoration, Stendhal found a society 'profoundly ill at ease with itself'. Swiftly the King and his right-wing Catholic coterie tried to bring back much of the authoritarianism that had led his brother to the guillotine. 'If these gentlemen (the Liberals) had full freedom,' he argued, 'they would end by purging me as well.'

Little more than three decades were to pass between Waterloo and the next major upheaval in Paris, in 1848, which – with the departure of the 'Bourgeois King', Louis-Philippe – would bring the final extinction of the French monarchy. During those three decades, there would be two more major revolts in Paris. After each one, the proletariat, the poor and the revolutionaries of the Faubourg Saint-Antoine would feel that the bourgeois had cheated them out of their birthright, the gains of insurrection – as indeed they had after the Great Revolution itself. Nevertheless, there were elements under the Restoration that a distinguished British historian like Richard Cobb could find to justify it as 'the happiest period in the violent and intransigent history of modern France'. Prosperity returned, business flourished as France caught up with Britain's industrial revolution, and so did literature – under giants like Chateaubriand, Hugo and Balzac – and the arts.

Louis XVIII would die painfully of gangrene only nine years after his restoration – the last French king to die while still on the throne, but mourned only in retrospect. His brother, the unpopular and reactionary Charles X, the last of the Bourbons, would be deposed in 1830, after just six years' rule. (In private, admiringly, he would refer to Napoleon as *Le Maître*, but it did him little good.) One more monarch, Louis-Philippe, would be unseated to join the lugubrious procession of French sovereigns into English exile in 1848. Over the course of the fifty-six years following the definitive abdication of Napoleon I, Paris would know three more turbulent and bloody revolutions and one humiliating siege, followed by defeat and civil war. In fact it would take those three successive nineteenth-century revolutions – of 1830, 1848 and 1871 – to demonstrate this truth, that, as after 1793, once again the French bourgeoisie had won. Then, at last, a semblance of equilibrium or synthesis between rival factions, between Bonapartists and two kinds of monarchist, *Bourbonistes* and *Orléanistes*, and various kinds of republican, would finally be achieved under the Third Republic in 1871.

*

During the first six years of the new regime, Napoleon sat fretting, miserable and sick, a prisoner in wind-swept Longwood – recording his memoirs and rewriting history in anger and resentment. For the record, much of his *ex post facto* writings should, regrettably, be ignored, or at least read most critically. He had committed but few errors, he claimed repeatedly. 'I was deserted rather than betrayed,' he wrote in his *Memorial*; 'there was more weakness and perfidy around me: it was a denial of St Peter'. If it was not the feebleness of Man that had let him down, it was the brutal power of Nature, striking down his own extraordinary force with which Nature had endowed him:

> in the south it was the sea that destroyed me; and in the north it was the fire of Moscow and the ice of winter; so there it is, water, air, fire, all Nature and nothing but Nature; these were the opponents of the universal regeneration commanded by Nature herself! The problems of Nature are insoluble!

On 5 May 1821, just as summer was arriving at that bleak outcrop of rock in the south Atlantic, Napoleon died. Did he fall, or was he pushed? Nearly two centuries later, experts still argue, even more excitedly than ever before, rival theories as to whether he was poisoned or not. Arsenic traces found in a lock of his hair? Poison – or something to do with the hair unguent he used? If poison, then who? Even the strongest advocates of the poison theory tend to let Napoleon's British gaolers off the hook; poison not being the 'British way of death'. Chief suspect: his French aide, General Montholon, royalist and with the possible additional motive of jealousy – Mme de Montholon may conceivably have been the last woman to have graced the Emperor's lonely bed. But shall we ever know? And, in fact, does it now matter? From the standpoint of the legend, it was wicked enough of the evil British to condemn so fine a hero of France to so dread an imprisonment. Might it not have been more merciful, creating less trouble in years to come, to have put him before a firing squad – like Marshal Ney, 'the bravest of the brave', or the unhappy Duc d'Enghien?

When news reached Paris three weeks later, reactions were mixed. The Duchesse de Broglie noted that 'Many young people wear mourning bands on their arms', and found people gathering 'in crowds around the print shops'. Talma would never again act on 5 May. But there were also those who, like Lady Bessborough, found 'perfect Apathy of everyone high and low here', while one loyal general (Foy) was shocked to find deputies in the Chamber talking about it 'as if it were a matter of indifference'.

As disenchantment with successive regimes grew, however, so Napoleon was to grow in stature. Writers like Hugo and Balzac did much to help cultivate it – though later in his life Hugo was to become a passionate opponent of Napoleon III. François-Pierre-Guillaume Guizot, a balanced historian and political leader himself under Louis-Philippe, wrote of him: 'It is much to have been, simultaneously, a national glory, a revolutionary guarantee, and a principle of authority.' Between August and December 1830, no fewer than fourteen plays glorifying Napoleon and the Empire were performed in Paris. But no one person did more to refocus Napoleon in French minds and legend than his successor, Louis-Philippe, the ultimate King of France, by having him brought back to France (aboard a ship curiously called the *Belle Poule*) and reburied in December 1840, with utmost pomp and circumstance, in a special tomb beneath the Invalides. Fulfilling Napoleon's desire to be buried, 'on the banks of the Seine, midst the French people whom I love so well', it was partly an attempt (only temporarily successful) by the King to stave off Lamartine's dreadful threat of *La France s'ennuie* ('France is bored'), which hovered banefully over his throne. To compensate for the drabness of his own regime, he certainly pushed the boat out with an extravaganza that Napoleon himself would have respected.

It was all 'so fabulous', wrote Heinrich Heine, 'that one could hardly believe one's eyes, it seemed as if one were dreaming'. On top of the Arc de Triomphe – which Napoleon had never finished, leaving it to Louis-Phillippe – had been erected a massive plaster statue of the Emperor, decked out in his coronation robes, and flanked by statues representing War and Peace. All the way along the route, down the Champs-Élysées to the Concorde and over the Seine to the Invalides, there were gilded Napoleonic eagles and flags and boards bearing the details of Napoleon's victories. All Paris turned out for the spectacle, with balconies rented out for as much as ff3000. Shortly after midday, the cortège, with the coffin borne in a huge coach drawn by sixteen horses clad in cloth of gold, reached the Invalides. Victor Hugo, letting himself go, wrote in *Choses vues*: 'An immense murmur enveloped this apparition . . .' It was 'as if the chariot were trailing the acclamation of the entire city, as a torch trails its smoke'. Amid cries, not heard for many a year, of 'Vive l'Empereur!' and 'À bas les anglais!' there were dissenters in the Paris crowd that day – but they were few. It was brave of the legitimist newspaper, *La Mode*, to question: 'what madness drives men to make heroes in this world of those who seem rather to have been sent by God to punish them?'

The stage was now set for Napoleon's successor as Emperor, his nephew – and an even greater disaster. It would be left to Louis-Napoleon, with Baron Haussmann, to complete his uncle's plans for reconstructing Paris and to transform the capital into roughly what it is today. Great works, and even greater ambitions – but at Sedan in September 1870 and Versailles the following January, Emperor Napoleon III would lead France to a defeat infinitely more humiliating than Waterloo; defeat by the very nation that Napoleon I had created, and one that exposed all Europe to the most terrible threat in its history, from across the Rhine.

*

What, then, could one say was the legacy left by the Age of Napoleon? The most important bequest of the French Revolution was the notion of social equality, and the abolition of privilege; Napoleon picked up this relative equality, imparting an imperial flavour to it which even the Restoration hesitated to touch. Napoleon defended freedom of worship, and did much to emancipate the Jews. He created, at least territorially, a united France out of the fragmented 'little nations' that the revolution had inherited. Napoleon, declares André Maurois, 'believed in equality and did not believe in liberty; he praised the Revolution for having destroyed the monarchy and feudalism', but then, to suit his own ends, he replaced it with another kind of authoritarianism; an authoritarianism that would long continue to attract some French in difficult times to come. 'I have aroused all ambitions, rewarded all merits, pushed back the frontiers of glory! All this is indeed something!' wrote Napoleon from St Helena. Yes, indeed; but over the years ahead the pursuit of *la gloire* would lead France into unattended trouble and terrible crises.

Down through the ages and across the world, Napoleon continues to fascinate and perplex. Many would feel like the Belgian industrialist, Moore, in Charlotte Bronte's *Shirley*: 'It puzzled me to this day how the conqueror of Lodi should have condescended to become an emperor, a vulgar and stupid humbug.' Inevitably dictators in the evil twentieth century, like Hitler, Stalin and Mao, as well tin-pot demagogues in Africa and South America, reach out to his image; yet, if compared with the monstrosities perpetrated by Hitler or Stalin, or even with the record of Louis XIV, Napoleon's 'crimes' retreat into insignificance. Writers like Thomas Carlyle would recognise the 'fatal moral flaw' in him – yet admire him as 'our last Great Man'. In America, the most influential writer of the nineteenth century, Ralph Waldo Emerson, would see in him the model of the 'self-made man'; while, so Paul Johnson reminds us, in

Britain authors as diverse as 'Belloc and Chesterton, Hardy and Shaw, hailed the Napoleon of legend variously as "the saviour of Europe", the emperor of the people, and the true superman'.

Legend is one thing, legacy another. Though he adopted and modified the centralisation imposed on France by Richelieu and Louis XIV, it was Napoleon's Civil Code and its various adjuncts that – for better or for worse – would stand the test of time and become the Mosaic tablets of the bureaucrats of twenty-first-century Brussels. Seeing today the realisation of so much of Napoleon's social agenda for Europe, it might be thought that it was Napoleon – not Wellington – who won on the slopes of Mont Saint-Jean. Above all, in the words of J. Christopher Herold, it remains 'impossible to enter that man's tomb without experiencing poignant emotion. His fatal attraction remains alive, even to those who would defend themselves against it ... What an artist! What deception.'

Bibliography

At the last count, there were over 600,000 titles dealing with Napoleon. Out of this huge bibliography, inevitably, I drew some material from my own two books on Napoleon; while Lanzac de Laborie provided me with a rare find. His eight volumes *Paris sous Napoléon* were published in Paris between 1900 and 1913, incomplete by the beginning of the First World War. Written a century after the events it describes, it reads with remarkable freshness and little prejudice. Marvellously well researched, amusing, and packed with marginal information about Napoleon's Paris, it is a real mine of information for scholars of the period. In England it appears to have been little read; the set I borrowed out of the London Library appears to have lain there dormant for the best part of a century, its pages still uncut.

The following works, listed in full below, are highly recommended for further reading and have been particularly useful: *The Terror Before Trafalgar* by Tom Pocock and *Daily Life in France Under Napoleon* by Jean Robiquet for their use of contemporary sources; *Napoleon and Josephine* by Evangeline Bruce, an outstanding recent biography which portrays their complex relationship with sensitivity; *Napoleon and English Romanticism* by Simon Bainbridge, to whom I am indebted for thoughtful surveys of contemporary attitudes of the English 'Romantics'; *The Making of the Poets* by Ian Gilmour, which also describes the situation in England; *Paris Between Empires* by Philip Mansel and *The Road to Waterloo* by Gregor Dallas, which are both entertaining and important accounts of this period; *Napoleon* by Paul Johnson; *A History of France* by André Maurois; and *The Age of Napoleon* by J. Christopher Herold.

Abrantes, Duchess, *Memoires*, Paris, 1895.
Aulard, F. A. *Paris sous le Premier Empire. Recueil de documents pour l'histoire de l'esprit public à Paris*, Paris, 1912.

Bainbridge, S., *Napoleon and English Romanticism*, Cambridge, 1995.

Baring, M., *Have You Anything to Declare?*, London, 1936.

Barnett, C., *Bonaparte*, London, 1978.

Baudot, F., *Mémoire du Style Empire*, Paris, 1990.

Bentley, E. C., *The First Clerihews*, Oxford, 1982.

Bergeron, L., *L'Épisode Napoléonien*, Paris, 1972.

Bidou, H., *Paris*, London, 1939.

Biver, M.-L., *Le Paris de Napoléon*, Paris, 1963.

Broglie, Victor, Duc de, *Souvenirs, 1785–1870* (4 vols), Paris, 1886.

Brookhiser, R., *Gentleman Revolutionary, Gouverneur Morris*, New York, 2003.

Bruce, E., *Napoleon and Josephine: An Improbable Marriage*, London, 1995.

Chandler, D. G., *The Campaigns of Napoleon*, London, 1967.

Chaptal, J.-A.-C., *Mes Souvenirs sur Napoléon*, Paris, 1893.

Chateaubriand, Fr., *Mémoires d'outre-tombe* (3 vols), Paris, 1951.

Clunn, H., *The Face of Paris: The Record of a Century's Changes and Developments*, London, 1933.

Cobb, R., *Paris and its Provinces 1702–1802*, Oxford, 1975.

—— *The Police and the People: French Popular Protest 1789–1820*, Oxford, 1972.

—— *Tour de France*, London, 1976.

Cole, R., *A Traveller's History of Paris*, Gloucester, 1994.

Cooper, D., *Talleyrand*, London, 1932.

Dallas, G., *1815; The Roads to Waterloo*, London, 1996.

Dark, S., *Paris*, London, 1926.

Denon, D.-V., *Correspondance*, 2 vols, Paris, 1999.

—— *L'Œil de Napoléon* (catalogue), Paris (Louvre), 1999–2000.

Duffy, E., *Saints and Sinners: A History of the Popes*, London, 1997.

Dupeaux, G., *French Society 1789–1970*,

Ehrlich, B., *Paris on the Seine*, London, 1962.

Foy, Général, *Notes Autobiographiques* (3 vols), Paris, 1926.

Garrett, M., *George Gordon, Lord Byron*, London, 2000.

George, Mlle (ed. Paul Cheramy), *A Favourite of Napoleon, Memoirs*, London, 1909.

Gilmour, I. *The Making of the Poets: Byron and Shelley in their Time*, London, 2002.

Hazlitt, W., *Life of Napoleon Buonoparte*, London, 1828.

Heine, H., *Lutèce*, Geneva, 1979.

Herold, J. C., *The Age of Napoleon*, London, 1963.

Higonnet, P., *Paris: Capital of the World* (tr. Arthur Goldhammer), Cambridge, Mass., 2002.

Horne, A., *How Far from Austerlitz? Napoleon 1805–1815*, London, 1996.

—— *Napoleon, Master of Europe, 1805–7*, London, 1979.

—— *The Seven Ages of Paris*, London, 2002.

Hugo, V., *Choses vues 1830–1846*, Paris, 1972.

—— *Les Misérables* (2 vols), Paris, 1862.

Jack, B., *George Sand*, London, 1999.

Johnson, P., *Napoleon*, London, 2002.

Keats, J., *Stendhal*, London, 1994.

Laffont, R., *Paris and Its People*, Paris, 1958.

Las Cases, E., *Le Mémorial de Sainte-Hélène*, Paris, 1951.

Lavedan, P., *Nouvelle histoire de Paris: histoire de l'urbanisme de Paris*, Paris, 1975.

Laver, J., *The Age of Illusion: Manners and Morals 1750–1848*, London, 1972.

Leveson-Gower, Lord G., *Private Correspondence 1781 to 1821* (2 vols), London, 1899.

Lewis, G., *Life in Revolutionary France*, London, 1972.

Lewis, G., and Lucas, C., *Beyond the Terror: Essays in French Regional and Social History 1794–1815*, Cambridge, 2002.

Mansel, P., *Paris between Empires, 1814–1952*, London, 2001.

Maurois, A., *History of France*, Paris, 1949.

May, G., *Stendhal and the Age of Napoleon*, New York, 1970.

McPhee, P., *A Social History of France, 1780–1880*, London, 1993.

Menuret de Chaume, J.-J., *Essais sur l'Histoire médico-topographique de Paris*, Paris, 1804, 1899.

The Oxford Book of French Verse, Oxford, 1957.

The Oxford Companion to French Literature, Oxford, 1959.

Pocock, T., *The Terror before Trafalgar: Nelson, Napoleon, and the Secret War*, London, 2002.

Reichardt, J. F., *Vertrauten Briefe aus Paris, Geschrieben in den Jahren 1802 und 1803*, Hamburg, 1804.

Rémusat, C. de, *Mémoires de ma vie*, Paris, 1958.

Rice, H. C., *Thomas Jefferson's Paris*, Princeton, 1976.

Robiquet, J., *Daily Life in France under Napoleon*, London, 1962.

Rudé, G., *Revolutionary Europe 1783–1815*, London, 1967.

Sand, G., *Œuvres autobiographiques*, Paris, 1970–1.

Schom, A., *Napoleon Bonaparte*, New York, 1997.

Shepherd, W., *Paris, 1802 and 1814*, London, 1814.

Sparrow, E., *Secret Service: British Agents in France, 1792–1815*, London, 1999.

Sutcliffe, A., *Paris: An Architectural History*, New Haven, 1993.

Talleyrand, C. M. de, *Mémoires* (5 vols), Paris, 1891–2.

Thiers, A., *Le Consulat et l'Empire*, Paris, 1932.

Vallois, T., *Round and About Paris* (3 vols), London, 1995–7.

Weber, E., *Peasants into Frenchmen, the Modernisation of Rural France 1870–1914*, London, 1977.

West, A., *Mortal Wounds*, London, 1975.

Willms, J., *Paris: Capital of Europe from the Revolution to the Belle Epoque*, New York, 1997.

Zweig, S., *Joseph Fouché*, London, 1930.

Index